My Cuban Revolution

My Cuban Revolution

How Fidel Castro changed my life

Satya Brown

Realifepress
Vancouver, Canada

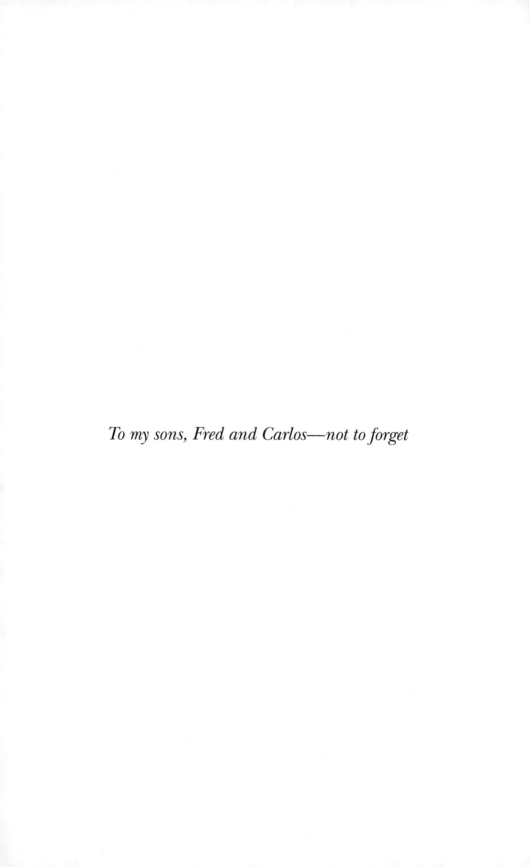

To my sons, Fred and Carlos—not to forget

Contents

Preface

Those Were the Times (For those who don't remember the 1950s)

Two memories stand out from my 1940s childhood in California.

When I was in second grade, the world had just witnessed the decimation of the Japanese city of Hiroshima by the atomic bomb. A million innocent people either died or were ill for the rest of their lives. Both the Americans and the Russians had the atomic bomb and threatened each other constantly, and their populations were hyped to live in fear. We were warned to be fearful. I remember that in school we were told, "If there is a bomb warning, you children have to instantly crawl under your desks." Sure.

Another memory. The Second World War was over, so my parents worked in the Army Surplus. One day they brought home a box of "wonderful papers" for us to use for painting. They were folded sheets thirteen by eighteen inches of thick, white paper, which seemed exciting. However, on the backside of each sheet was a poster that had about twenty photographs of miserable, starving children. It was frightening, and I vowed never to look at the backs of these sheets again. It did teach me a lesson early on: there were a lot of horrible things and famine in the world, and we were very lucky to be born where we were.

These memoirs describe the seventeen years, from 1962, to 1979, that I lived in Cuba, showing what life really was like in Cuba during those misunderstood years. Thist may be ancient history for some youngsters, but older folks will remember those times.. So that every reader can remember what was happening in the world in 1960, I will go backward, with a simplistic description of the world stage in the 1940s to the 1960s. That was many years ago. Human society has changed a lot, yet in other ways, the problems have stayed the same.

The First World War, from 1914 to 1918, resulted in the formation of most of our present European countries. In the United States, and partly in Canada, in the 1920s, the world was recuperating from war: there was food, trade, still vacant land, and a thriving stock market. A few individuals were becoming millionaires through different varieties of speculation.

Suddenly, at the end of the 1920s, the stock market crashed, wiping out the North American and European economies in seemingly contradictory conditions. There were products in the stores but no money to buy them. Since products didn't sell, manufacturing fell, and that meant the loss of jobs. Farmers couldn't sell their crops. This led to rotting food yet hunger. Some millionaires became paupers overnight and jumped to their deaths from high buildings.

I remember that at this time my father had a cattle ranch in Wyoming, and when his family couldn't sell the cattle, they transformed the ranch into a dude ranch for millionaires, which allowed the ranch to survive. They catered to those who were still millionaires, such as Nelson Rockefeller.

To make matters worse, the economy didn't seem to recuperate. The 1930s were known as the Great Depression—a time of joblessness and despair for the greater American population. Presidents and great economists shook their heads. It seemed that no one knew how to solve the contradictory economy.

Finally, a British economist named John Neville Keynes recommended that the government, in order to stimulate the economy, create jobs by borrowing money, amplifying the national debt. When I studied economy in my teens, I realized what he had done. The government was to borrow the money to pay for infrastructure jobs. This was called Keynesian economics, thus beginning the endless course of escalating government debt.

My parents and friends looked to the other side of the world, to a conglomeration of countries called the Soviet Union. The Soviets thought that they had a solution to eradicate poverty. The objective was to have the government control the economy so that there were neither rich nor poor and so that everyone could have equal access to resources. The concept was that as a citizen, you should "take what you need" and "give what you are able." This principle was named socialism and, more extremely, Communism. The idea was contagious and became widely spread, particularly among the poor and downtrodden. Even in the wealthier countries, for once the poor people envisioned having some control of their own governing.

The first country to embark on this theory was the Soviet Union. The Soviet Union was a combination of countries attached to Russia, all under this banner of Communism. There was no real map on how Communism should be run; the belief was that the government should control everything, so the Soviet government followed its own intuitions. With no Internet, practically no telephones, and poor mail service, any information about this country depended on the reporters who visited it. Some reporters were invited by the Soviet state. They gave glowing descriptions of wonderful collective farms, schools, and medicine for everyone. Other journalists reported terrorism under Stalin, lack of free speech, fear, and jailing of dissenters. Each side claimed that the other side was brainwashed. I imagine that both sides were right.

At the end of the thirties, the Second World War erupted. Germany, under Hitler, was at war with the rest of Europe. Now there were airplanes, with heavy machinery, and constant bombing. For everyone in Europe, it was a four-year nightmare that promised to go on and on. No one was winning. The United States was standing at the sidelines. After all, they had not been attacked, but Europe was begging for help. Not much later, the Japanese entered the war, hoping to control large portions of eastern Asia. On December 7, 1941, the Japanese bombed Pearl Harbor in Hawaii.

I was born on December 13, 1941, the same day that the Americans finally declared war. My parents, influenced by India's nonviolence advocate, Mahatma Gandhi, named me after his peace group, Satyagraha. The war was a wonderful way to justify government spending, to win at all costs, to spend, spend, spend, no questions asked. Young men were sent to die on the front, but everyone had jobs.

On the other hand, a number of intellectuals insisted (maybe rightly) that Hitler could have been stopped before the war, and they were horrified that the Americans had resorted to violence.

These people were called pacifists. They objected to all war, and during that time, pacifists who refused to fight, called conscientious objectors, were either jailed or given other jobs.

When the war ended, young men came home, married, and had families. The now-thriving economy supplied them with jobs and cute little bungalows. For a short while, all seemed well.

In North America and Europe, production and consumption increased; the rich got richer; and suddenly the men with the jobs found themselves getting poorer. There was no job security, no medical insurance, no old-age pensions, and no unemployment insurance. Hence, if a laborer lost a job, his family was ruined.

Workers protested, and stronger labor unions were organized, triggering off an even greater backlash. These activities caused numerous episodes of violence. Peaceful demonstrations for better conditions were met by police violence, and many union leaders were framed and jailed or murdered, causing fear to become part of our society. As a small child in California, as I lay in bed, I remember my parents and friends singing union protest songs.

The company "bosses" in the United States were so afraid of a strong working movement and so afraid that they could lose to Communism that what was nearly a reign of terror commenced. This war of words, spread by the media, kept the US and Russian populations in complete fear and was used by the governments to justify more arms buildup. This was called the Cold War, which lasted from the 1950s to the 1980s.

The FBI, under J. Edgar Hoover, was formed in the United States with the objective of spying on its own citizens. In the United States, there were courts whose aim was to call in "possible Communists," who might be anyone, to declare that they were loyal to the United States. They then had to give the name of any other "possible

Communist." If a defendant refused to give another name, he might be blacklisted and could lose his job. In that time, many Hollywood stars and producers were blacklisted. Freedom of speech underwent complete suppression. For some, democracy became a joke.

The Cold War was an attempt to combat Communism. The atom bomb had been invented and dropped on Hiroshima, killing hundreds of thousands, and now both sides were producing atom bombs. The Soviets were afraid that the Americans would attack them, maybe rightfully, so they geared up by producing arms. After all, they had just suffered a big invasion from the Germans. The Americans argued that the Soviets would attack them, which justified another huge buildup of arms. Each country taught its citizens to hate the other. The worst fear in the world was for a nuclear war.

Each country tried to stockpile more bombs than the other, more and more nuclear warheads, enough to blast thirty earths, and they didn't stop. The military buildup showed no signs of abating.

I once heard it described as two little boys standing in a garage, with three inches of gasoline on the floor, each one boasting who had the most number of matches.

The backlash from the Cold War, from the 1950s through the 1980s, activated an important element in the population—forming the peace movement. There were numerous peace marches, with hundreds to thousands of people carrying peace signs. They demonstrated at every opportunity where they seemed to find injustice.

My parents awoke early in those days and walked miles in these marches, doing their best to make a difference.

Internationally, other events were happening. Historically, in places such as Africa and Latin America, the land had been used by the indigenous people of the specific countries. Since writing was not a part of their lives, they never thought about having "land titles." It was simply their land as it had been for thousands of years. In the past two hundred years, different European "explorers" had taken over the easier overseas areas, establishing European cities, doling out portions of land titles to various individuals. The indigenous, without land titles, were ignored.

During this time, most Latin American countries were ruled by tyrants and dictators, favorable to money and more money, which came in the form of international investments. Foreign investors (mostly American corporations) were allowed unbridled control, causing devastating illiteracy and poverty and displacing whole villages of people, as if they didn't exist.

In the Latin American countries, the most common slogan was "Yanqui, go home!" Occasionally there were "elections," but if the elected government tried too hard to improve their people's economic condition (it was always at the expense of the foreign investors), the elected government was removed by a military coup, almost always funded and trained by the CIA. Thus there continued to be military dictatorships, and citizens continued to form gatherings, still shouting, "Yanqui, go home!"

I grew up in this period of oppression, when every-one had fear about speaking out. The nonconformists tended to group together, and a number came north to CanadaI with our family, guided by my father, Fred Brown. Without access to complete information (there was no such thing in those days), there were people who looked hopefully at the Soviet Union, thinking that the Soviets were the only ones really on the side of peace.

There was a dream.

For many centuries in history, people lived and died, accepting that the status quo "rich and poor" was how life was meant to be lived. Occasionally there were dreamers, with dreams, who dared to question the status quo, believ-ing that life could be better for everyone. Philosophers such as Aristotle were just talkers, but Plato wrote long polemics about how the world should be. Literate people at the time, who were just a few, nodded their heads at the great wisdom.

Nonetheless, a few dreamers were willing to act upon their dreams and actually attempt to change the world. These were often young men who had nothing to lose. In those days, "older folks" who had families to support were in their thirties or forties. Thus it was the younger men who succeeded in the French Revolution, the Russian Revolution, and the American Revolution. They say that it only takes 10 percent of the population to make a revo-lution. History is full of these attempts—some more and some less successful.

Where poor people are downtrodden, sooner or later they try to revolt. There were a lot of these people in the Western Hemisphere in the 1950s.

My father, classified as a "philosopher," spent his life trying to counteract the negative aspects of the consumer society by forming intentional communities in the hinterland, as he experimented with different forms of community life.

In this, my memoirs of Cuba, I describe the efforts of some of the dreamers.

One

My Pivotal Birthday

The chance meeting:

It was the evening of my twenty-first birthday. December 1962.

I had always envisioned that my twenty-first birthday would be a significant step for me. It would be the beginning of my life, and I took the concept of life very seriously. Throughout my childhood, my unconventional parents had moved us in and out of a long line of different locations, exposing us to numerous, contrasting North American communities and lifestyles, and never viewing "stability" as a necessary consideration. Stability was to be a part of one's inner life view, not a factor in external living conditions.

From a young age, living in Canada, I viewed the whole human race as part of my family, and life was about doing a small part in improving any ills in the world. "Making a living" and "having a family" were taken for granted.

I was excited foreseeing what would be my role in the world, and I was taught that it was possible to do anything, but preparation was the key in getting on in life.

Thus, at the age of twenty, having taught school and saved some money, I had decided to visit the newly established social regime in the nearby island of Cuba. There were a good number of Canadians, Americans and observers from other countries who were welcomed in Cuba, since the Cubans wanted the outside world to see what they were really achieving. Many of these foreigners often got jobs making use of their expertise. My intention was to observe this social phenomena for several months, then return to Canada to continue studies of political science. Little did I realize that an unexpected meeting that same evening would alter all of these plans for my future.

Even with this thought in mind, little did I realize that a stupendous direction would begin on my twenty-first birthday.

My friends had just taken me to a concert featuring a talented Soviet violinist and the Cuban Symphony Orchestra. Now the six of us were squished into a mini–station wagon, cruising the quiet night streets, deciding what to do next. However, I was not with my lifelong friends, cruising familiar streets in my own city of Vancouver in Canada. I was with newfound friends, cruising the streets of Havana, Cuba, where I had been for five months.

A plump, feisty Canadian woman, Bella Stall, was driving her cramped mini–station wagon. Many Canadians and Americans had come to Cuba in the past year, with the intention of giving technical assistance to the new Cuban government. ~~Bertha~~ *Bella* was in Cuba to help direct education, working directly in the Education Ministry. . Her thin, scholarly-looking husband and her fortunately skinny brother-in-law both sat upright in the front passenger seat. Three of us ladies were squished into the backseat. Elegant, twenty-year-old Carmen had become a close friend when I first became acquainted with *repatriados*, who spoke both English and Spanish. A repatriado was a person who had previously left Cuba for the United States to escape the vicious, bloodthirsty dictator Batista, and then returned as soon as Fidel's Cuban Revolution ousted Batista. Carmen's large, jolly mother sat in the backseat, and I was the third. This tight togetherness erupted in lots of laughter.

We were all laughing and joking; we were all in a state of euphoria. Why was this motley group all in Cuba at this time? All six of us wanted to experience the new revolution. We all felt as if we were at the brink of a monumental world challenge, a change that might lead the way to a fairer world. In many people's minds, there was no doubt that all of the intentions of the Cuban Revolution would be an absolute success.

Although sharing their happiness and hope, I was there only to observe. Even at the age of twenty, I had studied a lot of history and sociology, aware that the best-laid plans had many bumps on the road, but I was excitedly optimistic that with good intentions, many monumental improvements could be effected.

Satya Brown

In 1962, the tiny, Spanish-speaking island of Cuba, just ninety miles from the United States, was the center of attention in the press, among capitalists and Communists, in daily conversation, and in people's minds. In 1959, with the promise of equality and eradicating poverty, a young, bearded man, always in a simple dark-green uniform, Fidel Castro, had organized a ragtag army of peasants and poor people. They then marched from the eastern mountains, crossed the country to the capital, Havana, and ousted the odious dictator, Batista. They took over the Cuban government, with Fidel Castro, an idealistic, optimistic, extremely charismatic young man, as prime minister.

Revolutions in Latin American countries were not rare. One leader would oust another, and sooner or later, the country's economic situation would stay the same. Promises, promises, but no action. To the world's amazement, Fidel suddenly began introducing earthshaking changes.

It wasn't long before Fidel set laws that every person should have a house, and the owners of ten houses realized that it might not go well for them. There was an immediate exodus of rich and upper-middle-class citizens who abandoned their houses and furniture but scooped up all their money and moved to Miami. Not much later the new government nationalized all foreign property in Cuban territory, triggering off a break in Cuban-American relations and prompting the United States to create a worldwide economic blockade against Cuba.

Fidel promised free education at all levels, free medical treatment, and affordable housing, and to the world's surprise, he was on his way to keep those promises. Half the world cheered, half the world feared. What was happening?

In the United Nations, in September 1961, Fidel declared, "We are neither capitalist nor Communist; we are humanists." Unfortunately, as the United States stopped all trade, and the Soviet Union offered its friendship, the Cuban Revolution had to declare itself as Communist. However, in every Cuban heart, there was determination for their way to be entirely different from the Soviet way.

Thus, the six of us were riding Bella Stall's little cantankerous vehicle into the future. It was eleven o'clock at night after the concert, and the streets were empty. We were in the newer, luxurious area of "uptown" called La Rampa. There were only sporadic lights on in the roadside medium-sized apartment buildings. The few streetlights were dim, allowing the brilliant sky to sparkle with the stars and moonlight, and outlining the black palm trees and the square shape of buildings against it. As Bella drove, the wide boulevard seemed to shimmer like a silver ribbon flowing underneath us. The air was just cool, but not cool enough for sweaters yet. It felt like paradise.

Cruising up Calle G, as Bella turned left onto Twenty-third Avenue, we all noticed a large, square window lit up in the dark background. Yay, an open restaurant. No sooner had we noticed that when our eyes looked downward, and we caught sight of the bright blue car, the only 1960 Chevrolet in Cuba—Fidel's car, with the requisite black Fiats of his entourage behind it.

"Oh!" we all cried in unison.

"Fidel is in that restaurant," exclaimed Bella, starting to pull her car toward the curb. "Shall we go inside? Let's see if we can get a glimpse of Fidel."

There was no instant reply.

With a lot of discussion about the appropriateness of the decision, we continued traveling roughly another ten blocks. I felt very hesitant. I wanted to meet Fidel someday, but not just in a lineup for a handshake. However, the majority voted otherwise, so Bella did a U-turn, and we returned to the restaurant.

It appeared to be open, so we parked and walked in. It was a large, white, barren-walled space, with white tablecloths set for the next day. There were few other customers, but eventually they left, leaving us alone in the empty room. The few employees were huddled together, chatting softly, in the rear kitchen. We saw a small closed door near the restaurant's entrance, with a relaxed, lone military guard who gave us a slight nod and smile. It looked as if Fidel and his friends were in an adjacent room, maybe looking at a floor show.

Finally a waiter showed up, and we each ordered ice cream, which they seemed to have available. Then we waited and waited, but there was no movement from the adjacent room.

"How will we get his attention?" murmured Carmen. Silence, everybody was thinking.

Then Bella announced, "Let's forget about this whole business and go to my place. I just prepared a special Jewish dish, and we'll all eat it."

Then it dawned on us! Bella grabbed a slightly dirty napkin, pulled out a pen, and scribbled a note saying that we were three Canadians wanting to meet him and that we would like to invite him to join us tonight for a special Jewish dinner. We beckoned the sheepish guard to our table, and in mangled Spanish, Bella explained that she wanted the note carried to Fidel now.

Then we waited again, but fairly soon the guard came out and said, "He will see the Canadians." Of course, all six of us crowded to the door.

As we pushed through the small door, feeling petrified, I was first and found my face propelled against the chest of the ubiquitous dark-green uniform. I looked upward, and a smiling, bearded face was looking down at me and shaking my hand. Amazed. I realized that this was *the* Fidel. He was a normal six feet tall but appeared so *big* (I guess most Cubans are shorter).

He was in a smaller, almost empty, dimly lit room, with a group of people around one table, chatting quietly and drinking beer. The rest of our tongue-tied group entered, considering what to say. But Fidel, a great diplomat, began to ask us questions. He invited us for a beer and had us sit down with the group. Right away Fidel started to boast about how well he could cook pasta.

"What is this special Jewish dish that you mentioned?" Fidel asked. "I'm a good cook myself. I want to know all about it."

A big discussion about food started, with Fidel and Bertha, in mangled Spanish, boasting about the entrées they could cook and what ingredients they used. Fidel just drooled, and his eyes popped open when she described her recipe. I thought he was so cute! His gestures and actions were just like a big kid. We roared with laughter throughout our conversations.

We were introduced to the rest of the group, which included the young, greasy chap, Joaquin, head of the university student union, and Fidel's right-hand man—Comandante Rene Vallejo. Although he was only in his forties, Vallejo already had pure white hair and a straggly white beard. He spoke to us in perfect American English and in many cases served as Fidel's translator. I later learned that he was a physician and had served as the doctor when the soldiers were grouping in the mountains, but he really was a practicing gynecologist. The rest of the group consisted of some guards. We were introduced to a quiet, well-dressed, educated young woman. I forget what her title was, but she didn't stay with the group for long.

Eventually Fidel announced, "All this talk about food is making me hungry. Let's go to Bella's house and eat!" We all jumped into our cars, and away we went—an impressive flotilla through the night, with us leading Fidel.

Bella's apartment building, in typical Cuban style, was three stories high, each floor a separate apartment, with an exterior stairway leading to each one. This particular building was very modern 1950s style, mainly consisting of polished, dark wooden beams and lots of enormous glass windows. Very classy.

When we reached the building, some guards surrounded the place, and then we climbed the plank stairs with Fidel and his three close buddies right behind us. Wow, if only the neighbors in the adjacent apartments had known!

Generally, one was in great awe of Fidel, but once we were with him, it didn't feel that way. He made us feel completely at ease and relaxed immediately. He liked joking around; his talk was familiar; and he treated everyone as if he were a special friend.

Instantly, Bella escaped to the kitchen and began pulling all the dishes out of her refrigerator. Pots and pans were banging, as she set to cook. The rest of us roamed around the fancy, well-decorated apartment, with objects from all over the world. The furniture boasted a number of bright colors, and paintings on the wall were from many countries. Dutch glass doors led the way to an unlit, spacious balcony, surrounded by a mixture of palm trees and fir trees. Fidel strolled out, observing everything as he moved, and I quickly trailed behind him.

We conversed in Spanish.

"Your Spanish is quite good," he told me as he stretched his arms on the balcony railing. I didn't tell him that I'd studied Spanish for two years—by correspondence—but never had a chance to hear it or use it. I must admit, my Spanish was never more fluent as that evening. I rattled on using words and structures that I never realized that I knew, and conversation flowed smoothly.

He asked about my work, because I had two jobs—one teaching English to high school students in Tarara, and an evening stint teaching English as a foreign language in the local language school called Abraham Lincoln. Tarara was a beach community about twenty minutes east of town, where the empty private homes were taken for boarding high school students—like a free private school. Several simple, new one-story buildings had been constructed to serve as classrooms—simple rooms with individual school desks, and a half-wall of wooden-shuttered windows—with no heating and no air conditioning. I remembered that the students were polite, but not particularly interested in learning English. The teaching style was a new technique, mainly in the form of group repetition of sentence structure. A group of us had taken a special course previously on how to use this technique.

"I am very interested in what is happening in Tarara," said Fidel. "It is a pet project of mine, and my son is studying there. Did you know that all those students didn't go to school last year, but worked as teachers? Each one was sent to live together in a peasant home, where they worked in the fields during the day, and then taught classes to the illiterate farmers in the evening, trying to get them to a grade three level. Most of these people had never had a chance to read and write, but I want everyone in Cuba to be literate. All education will be free all the way through university. Most of these little straw huts did not have electricity, so they had to teach with kerosene lamps. All of these students, and many more, were my heroes."

Fidel was highly emotional about this epic year. It had been a priority, and it was a blazing success story. All the participants, almost the entire population, either taught or studied, and the collective pride was palpable.

Then Fidel wanted to emphasize his dreams for a new Cuba: to provide jobs and equality for everyone, to eliminate homelessness, to eliminate poverty, to give free medical attention to each person, to provide free education for every citizen, and to maximize the agriculture in the lush countryside. Of course, this sounded like utopia, but he was excitedly optimistic about reaching many of his goals.

To tell the truth, since the world powers were not getting it right in their efforts to decrease poverty, any new steps were interesting, and I was in Cuba to see how their efforts would take place. I was young, and I could feel the intense excitement in these young people, and their enthusiasm and optimism were rubbing off on me. I was eager to observe these wonders evolve.

Fidel particularly expounded on one of latest plans to develop his expansive ideas. "There must be many young Western graduates in every facet of science and economics who would be willing to work here a few years and help us with their expertise. We need foreign technicians, teachers, and scientists to help us. If you know of any such persons, or can put the word out, we would be very appreciative."

At that time, there were a good number of Soviet "experts" living the good life in Cuba, but unfortunately they were not as knowledgeable about Western standards, which Cuba did understand. A lot of their suggestions were not compatible with the Cuban culture and expectations.

Oh, my heart was racing. My father—a philosopher, teacher, and jack-of-all-trades—was dreaming of coming to Cuba, to write or teach philosophy. Dare I bring it up? This was certainly the right moment.

"Well, my father is a philosopher and a teacher, he is very interested in what Cuba is doing, and he would be only too happy to work in the university here." I explained about my dad's degrees and background, which was definitely far from ordinary. My father Fred Brown, at that time teaching high school, had his philosophy degrees from the Chicago University, plus an in-depth understanding of many of the current pragmatic philosophies. In Cuba, my father would be studying and evaluating the new concepts and social plans.

"*Es un problema resuelto*" exclaimed Fidel. "It's a problem already solved. Cuba needs exactly that, philosophy professors who are open to new thoughts. We could use an English teacher in the Isle of Pines. It's a gorgeous place, but I think he'll be needed at the university first. We'll be in touch with you."

Sure, of course I had to see it to believe it, but I admit that I was dumbfounded and elated. Pinch me. Was this really happening? My father's dream? Everyone said that Fidel remembered everything, and I'd seen verification of this, but still.

Then Fidel flattered me about how well I was using Spanish. I guess there was hope for me. My first important conversation in Spanish. Soon afterward, Carmen came to the balcony, and we chatted about everything from buses to houses, from hairstyles to love. Let's face it—these Latin Cubans consider themselves great lovers. The younger man with Fidel's group, Joaquin, was drooling all over me. He wanted to dance with me, but I found him a bit icky, so I was unmoved. Of course, I was kidded a lot, because a young *soltera* (single girl) alone in Cuba was something special.

"The one thing Cuba is now producing a lot," announced Fidel, "is matrimony."

In Fidel's group, Comandante Vallejo attracted my attention. He was a bit older than the others. (To young people, a person in his or her forties is older.) He kept chewing on his long white beard. Since his English was perfect, he and I discussed music, as he used to play the piano. He kept putting more records on the record player. He mentioned that he had a son in school with me, just as Fidel had.

Fidel sat in the biggest wicker chair, spreading his huge legs over the adjacent chairs. He laughed and joked and popped into the kitchen to test the dishes. He thought everything needed eggs.

"Next time I come to this house," he asserted, "which will be soon, I will do the cooking. But I can't do anything without eggs." Then he turned to his aide, "Make sure that this senora always has lots of eggs in this house."

We had a wonderful dinner together, but Fidel had to remove his feet from the chairs, because there weren't enough seats for everyone.. He hollered because his plate wasn't big enough but then refused a larger plate. Later he was intrigued by a large pair of garden clippers and, like a typical kid, started to cut his fingernails with them.

I admonished him. "Remember, your fingers are useful for some things."

He answered, "I don't need fingers. My principal function is to talk."

His eyes always twinkled; he moved his arms and head like a big boy. He wasn't really extremely tall or fat, but he really seemed larger than life. And man, he had some flashy boots!

He tested the spaghetti to see when it was ready, watched the biscuits baking, and kept an eye on everything else.

The Castro group stayed until about four thirty in the morning, and he promised to visit Bella again. He confided to me that she was one of the most simpatico people he had ever met. We could barely stay awake, and his poor guard, really a sweet fellow, could hardly keep his eyes open.

They said that Fidel generally had a new set of "buddies" every month because he really burned them out. They just couldn't keep up with him, and I believed it. The people affectionately called him the *caballo* (the horse) because he was so strong. There was nothing like getting everything from the horse's mouth.

Carmen's mother drove me home—home being a bedroom in a sprawling, luxurious ranch that the owner had fled, where young, identical military twins with their girlfriends had each taken a bedroom. I was offered the empty, spacious fourth bedroom, which I happily accepted. Jose, an old, old man, had been taking care of the house for sixty years and continued to care for it.

I was too wound up to sleep, so I sat down at my desk.

Wow! What had just happened! Was I dreaming? I had spent my childhood preparing for life. All these years my parents had dedicated themselves to giving me the best, broadest, and most worldly education possible. Now would I be able to start helping them back?

I started writing a letter to my dad. I described the evening, but I kept repeating that he would have to see it to believe it. It was almost too good to be true.

I finished my letter about Fidel, and I told my dad about how Fidel said he now considered us to be among his best personal friends. And he was just like an ordinary friend. It seemed hard for me to believe that this jolly fellow with the easygoing personality was the giant who had led a country to do the impossible, one of the world's greatest leaders. I guess that's what made him so fantastic.

We were so young. I was twenty-one, and Fidel was thirty-six. Here we were, planning on improving the lives of a whole nation—a very tall order. We were the dreamers.

Continuing encounters:

Monday evening, three days after my encounter with Fidel, I arrived home from work exhausted and threw all my papers on the bed. To my surprise, at ten o'clock that night, old Jose knocked on my door.

"Satya. There's a telephone call for you!"

I'd never had a telephone call before. In fact, I didn't even know there was a telephone in the house and certainly had never given the number to anyone. A little warily, I picked up the phone.

"*Hola*," I managed to say.

"Hello, Satya" came a man's voice in perfect English. "I'm calling for the people you were with the other night, about that topic."

What? I wondered.

"Yes, with Fidel. This is Vallejo. I want to discuss the arrangements for your parents to come to Cuba."

I was flabbergasted. Pinch me. This couldn't be true.

"Are you going to be there awhile?" he continued. "Don't go to bed yet. We'll be there right away."

I told Jose that Fidel would be here in a few minutes, but he wouldn't believe me.

Sure enough, at 10:45 p.m., several Jeeps drove into the driveway, and Fidel and Vallejo calmly entered our house. Although a number of my roommates already knew Fidel, but the others were completely stunned. They raved about how I had deserved two visits with Fidel in three days. Truthfully, I was stunned too.

"I need your parents' address and phone number." Fidel explained how he'd visited the Ministry of Education that morning, where they had evaluated job possibilities for Dad.

Fidel continued. "Are there other members of your family who need to be invited? We'll bring your mother, your sister. Is there anyone else? How can we notify them, and when will they be able to come? Our Cuban embassy in Canada will make all the arrangements."

Yes, I thought, my parents lived at the end of the world. They were teaching in Telegraph Creek, near the Yukon border. It was literally the end of the world—no mail, no telephone, with minimal communication possibilities. Fidel reassured me that they would find a way to communicate (dog sled?), and they were ready to bring my family as soon as they could. Yes, he said, bring the dogs, bring any cars, bring all of our belongings.

Vallejo read some of the poems that my father had written and sent to me and said he loved them.

After chatting with the gathering, I sneaked into my room—another letter to write! My insides were jumping up and down with excitement. I kept repeating, "My God, I'm the luckiest girl on earth and getting luckier by the minute!" Even though I'd heard that Fidel was a stickler for detail, I was astounded that, with a whole country to run, he had remembered our situation.

Much later, I learned about the "notification" in the isolated, redneck town of Telegraph Creek. The town was an Indian reservation "ruled" by the RCMP officer who had the only phone in town. This was during the Cold War period, and the cop's job was to quash and thwart any existing "Communists," which he could interpret to be anybody he wanted. Imagine the situation where he had to find my dad and tell him that the Cuban embassy was calling.

A few nights later, as I returned from work, old Jose came running to my room. The whole household, many of Fidel's friends, had been waiting for me.

"Satya, a jeep came and left something for you!" Old Jose showed me a huge basket full of wines, cheeses, *turrones* (Spanish Christmas candy), and tins of special condiments.

"That's not all," announced Jose. He opened the freezer and showed me a thirty-pound turkey. A card in the basket read, "Compliments of Fidel Castro. Merry Christmas." Everyone hugged me with surprise and excitement.

Although they all wanted to eat it with me, in reality they all had other commitments, so I shared my goodies at a big Christmas party in Carmen's mother's house.

A few weeks later, I was standing at a bus stop on the beautiful Miramar Boulevard, enjoying the palm trees skirted by the lush green lawn swaying against the blue sky. I was planning to meet up with some friends in the central Habana Libre Hotel, where we often met for drinks. (My drinks were only soft.) I waited and waited and waited, much longer than an hour, but not one single bus passed.

As I was getting tired standing, suddenly a group of cars passed me—a blue Chevrolet and two black Fiats. I immediately recognized Fidel's entourage. As they reached the next corner, the cars stopped and backed up to where I stood.

"Satya, where are you going?" Fidel reached out the window to shake my hand.

"To the hotel Habana Libre, but no buses have passed."

"Get in," said the driver of the second car. "Fidel told me to take you where you need to go." And they did.

A couple of weeks later, I met Lucila. She was Tony's girlfriend—Tony being one of the young military men in my house. She was living in a big house all alone after her parents had fled to the United States. She invited me to live with her, which was wonderful for both of us. I was given a cool, spacious bedroom and a bathroom, both with marble floors. (In the fifties, having a balcony was the ultimate in luxury.) In the mornings I worked in Tarara, the distant boarding high school at the beach, and now, in the evenings, I had a job teaching English in the Havana language school, called Abraham Lincoln. This meant getting home at about 10:30 p.m.

On several occasions, Fidel and a couple of his friends would show up at Lucila's house at eleven o'clock at night (after a hard day of work?), and we'd all sit around having coffee and discussing philosophy, politics, or current events. Lucila's Spanish, of course, was better than mine, so she sometimes dominated the conversation.

On one of these occasions, Fidel chatted with me at length about one of his new plans. He wanted to promote Canadian tourism in Cuba, which could become an ideal industry, but at the moment, the Americans would not let Canadian airlines fly over the United States if they were headed to Cuba—a small detail to overcome. He had hopes that I could be a liaison in this new project when it came into place, which led to interesting discussions.

On a sunny April afternoon, as I sat reading on my balcony, a Jeep roared into our driveway and screeched to a stop. Vallejo!

"Satya, jump in! We have to find a house! Your parents will be arriving next week."

Wow, I hadn't heard anything more about the invitation because communication was so extremely difficult. Now my family was almost here.

He drove me to a neat, middle-class suburb called Nuevo Vedado to show me a couple of houses. Calle Norte, the street, was a horseshoe shape that had once been a quarry—hence a roundabout with big cliffs behind it. The first house was typical Spanish, with many little rooms and little useless corners. All the houses were made of stucco, with highly polished, marble-like floors, or tiles. I shrugged my shoulders, so he wanted to take me to another house across the street.

The new house looked as if it were made of square gray block, but there were lots of glass windows. On entering, I saw a large open area that would serve as the front room, dining room, and family room—what we would now call "open concept" but was rare in those days. It had polished granite floors, a wall of glass slats, and a middle stairway of shiny wooden boards, with a skylight and a garden below. One wall was completely made of wooden-slatted panels, all of which could open the whole wall to the outside of the house. There were three spacious bedrooms, three modern bathrooms, and lots of closets, even by today's standards.

When one opened the wooden wall, next to the house was an empty lot. "What will happen to this lot? Who will live beside me?" I asked.

Vallejo looked it over. He replied, "Take it!"

And we did.

Two

My Unconventional Childhood

Born to be different:

Iwas born on December 13, 1941. The Japanese had bombed Pearl Harbor on December 7, but the thirteenth was the exact day that the Americans declared war. My parents were die-hard pacifists, and that the United States would go to war was a huge shock to them. They thoroughly believed with India's Gandhi that nonviolence and peaceful civil disobedience were the only way to solve the world's problems. They named me after Gandhi's peace force, *Satyagraha*. I was told that *Satya* meant "truth." Taking me and my siblings with them, my parents dedicated their lives to studying the complex world of truth.

My father, Fred Brown, a direct descendant of the inspirational American hero John Brown, was an explorer and a dreamer. When I was a child, I had asked "what" my father was, and I was told that he was a philosopher. He insisted that happiness was not bought with money but depended on a caring relationship among all members of society. At that time in history, the Soviet Union had formed a Communist government in which all members of society were to be equal. All industry and production was controlled by the state in order to guarantee equality. Many reporters visited and returned with glowing tales of beautiful schools, farms, and day cares; and other reporters told of oppression and horrors. I believe they were both correct. My father, with theories about the best ways for people to share their lives and the best ways to eliminate the competitive rat race, repeatedly experimented with organizing intentional communities.

We moved from one place to another, with my father's intention of organizing communities based on cooperation, not greed. When we were children, our parents took me, together with one brother and one sister, to Wyoming, San Francisco, and then to the Canadian hinterland of British Columbia—homesteading in the isolated mountains near Smithers. His plan was that other people would follow us there to form a community, which could only succeed if it was far enough away from greedy, competitive civilization. Smithers was already at the end of the world, and we moved twenty miles into the wilderness. If that wasn't far enough away from the influences of civilization, I don't know where that could be. A small sawmill located itself on our land, paying stumpage for our trees, and sometimes was a source of paying jobs.

Eventually, some other people joined us and built shacks in our settled area.

Wilderness child:

My unusual childhood started in this peaceful, distant wilderness tucked between the mountains.

"Well, Satya," my father often philosophized to me, "there are many things that must be corrected on this earth." I was ten years old and nodded my head like an obedient puppy.

We were sitting on a comfortable log, enjoying the cool spring sunshine in our isolated forest homestead. We had made a clearing for our overfeatured "shack," our beautiful cull-lumbered, slab-decorated home, surrounded by goats, sheep, dog, and cats. Between the melting snow patches, the fresh, green leaves of shrubs and grass were now happily sprouting from the mud. The closest neighbors were two miles away, where the tiny sawmill was now located.

"There are lots of thinkers in this world, " he continued, "but the most important consideration, besides studying and thinking, is doing something to follow your beliefs."

"A foolish consistency is the hobgoblin of little minds," he would say. (He liked to quote Emerson.) "Just remember, Satya. It may be important to talk, but in life, you must *do* your beliefs. If you change your mind, and then believe another way, then change your direction. That's all right."

Even though he prided himself on being a profound thinker, his favorite phrase was this: "Give me a man who can do something." He himself was a jack-of-all-trades—skier, cattleman, mountaineer, philosopher, builder, teacher, and university professor.

We children were given everything to do—lumber, nails, hammers, paints, saws, books. We built our own tree houses and playhouses, and we made our own toys—doll beds, wooden chainsaws, and I wrote poetry, plays, and stories, of course, at the fifth-grade level. My brother and I were free to explore the grand, natural world. We could run forever, jump in streams, dive into secret hide-outs in the forest, care for the animals, and play with rocks and plants.

For two years, people came to our community, many of them from Berkeley, California. Unfortunately, personal relationships were again the downfall of the community.

Instead of thinking in terms of failure, my father went on to explore more dreams. In the middle of these adventures, there was still the necessity of "making a living," so my father became a schoolteacher, working in a different town every two years. I never established roots, but I hardly noticed. Stability in our world was only within our tight-knit family.

I continued in high school, every year a different school or correspondence course. In 1959, I graduated from Ft. Saint John High School with honors. I remember receiving a scholarship from the Alumni of the University of British Columbia. Wearing a new dress, I went to a fancy reception in the university hall and had my first glimpse of what the other half of the world looked like.

Now on my own:

Now graduated from high school, I knew that *life* was to begin. The whole world was before me, and I felt that every option was open to me. I never thought about making more money or living in fancier houses. I wanted to do something useful, something that would be my little effort to better the world. The first step would be to go to a university, to learn.

That summer vacation, in 1959, my brother and I had free time. In a quirky setup, my brother and I had bought a new car, a little Renault Dauphine. I was seventeen years old, and my brother was sixteen. We put our accordion and guitar on a roof rack, and then together we drove all across the United States to Maine, then back through Canada (before the Trans-Canada Highway was built), visiting relatives, and putting ten thousand miles on the car before we made the first payment.

After one year of teacher training at UBC, two summer school sessions, and many correspondence courses, I now had my teaching certificate. Together with my parents, I taught in a three-room school in Telegraph Creek. It was not only the farthest north, near the Yukon, but it also had the highest isolation pay in the province, including free housing and transportation. With this job, I was able to pay off all debts and save money quickly.

News seeps to the north:

This is what I was doing when the amazing news shook up our lives.

"Damn those Yankee bastards!" exploded my father as he set the dinner on the table. That spring of 1961, we were the three teachers in Telegraph Creek, and we took turns making dinner. When Dad cooked, the food was always baked. So we were served roasted moose meat and baked potatoes.

He finally settled down at the dining room table with us. Our cozy little log cabin, called "the teacherage," was tucked into the steep hillside overlooking tiny wooden shacks and a few "real houses" on the various plateaus. At nightfall our picturesque view was like an antique English painting: glittering silver forest, the meandering white river, all speckled with color from the dimly lit cottages.

"They tried to invade a beachhead in Cuba," Dad continued.

Cuba? Yes, Cuba.

Before 1960, most North Americans didn't even know where Cuba was. I knew that it was the weekend resort of American debauchery; after all, I'd seen the movie *Guys and Dolls* in which Marlon Brandon had coerced the pretty, religious lady to visit a nightclub in Havana, Cuba.

"Yes," Dad carried on, "they say that the Cuban Bay of Pigs was attacked by Cuban mercenaries from Miami, but I'll bet my bottom dollar that they were armed and financed by the American CIA. The Americans are just dying to establish a tiny foothold in Cuba, set up a dummy government, and recognize it as the legitimate one."

I had been living in Vancouver at the beginning of 1960, studying hard, and barely paying attention to the news, so my knowledge of Cuban events was minimal. In September 1960, the whole family had migrated back to Telegraph Creek, this time with me also working as a teacher. In that northern post, the occasional newspaper came three weeks late, and the only radio reception was blurry, inconsistent shortwave, making it very difficult to keep up with world news. My father spent long evenings bent over the radio, deciphering global events.

As of that dinner moment, I started to pay more attention to my father and the Cuban events.

I learned that, in a far-off island called Cuba, a young man named Fidel Castro had succeeded in ousting a bloodthirsty, cruel dictator Batista, who had been ruling for several years. This, in itself, was nothing new. Most Latin American countries were constantly having uprisings and counter uprisings to get rid of tyrants. The new governments would promise improvement for the poor and the hungry, but most times the new rulers would carry on business as usual, so they were allowed to remain. If the rebels tried to change the status quo, or make waves in the existing American-favored economy, the CIA would find a way to instigate a coup d'état, reinstalling new leaders more favorable to the American companies. Skeptical thinkers often called these new leaders "American puppets."

But to everyone's amazement (and to the horror of others), this new government was actually defying the foreign corporations, giving land to the farmers, and eliminating the slums.

From here on, my father and I dug for any information we could find—in the British *Guardian* newspaper, even reading the book *Cuba: Anatomy of a Revolution,* by Leo Huberman and Paul Sweezy. An American journalist, Herbert Mathews, met with Fidel frequently and wrote a series of articles in the *New York Times,* until the newspaper decided that it didn't want to know anymore. Little by little, the information came filtering in to us.

Here's what I learned.

Fidel Castro takes over the news:

Fidel Castro, law graduate from the University of Havana, had been very active in student rebellion against the odious Cuban Batista regime. Many of the activist students had been tortured and murdered by Batista's military during the fifties. (Two blocks from our house in Cuba, a military torture chamber had been torn down and made into a children's park. The stone base was all that remained.)

In 1953, Fidel organized a group of determined young people with plans to take over Batista's military fortress in the eastern province of Oriente. Fidel was such an enthusiastic and passionate leader that it was not difficult for him to enlist followers. These men and women trained themselves in military tactics, and on July 26, 1953, they attacked this *Cuartel Moncada* (the Moncada Barracks). Fidel's group lost, and many of them were murdered by Batista's army, and the rest, including Fidel, were sent to prison.

Ever since, July 26 has been considered the beginning of the Cuban Revolution. Eventually Fidel went to trial and was pardoned. Of significance in this trial, Fidel gave a long diatribe, published a thousand times in many languages, titled "History Will Absolve Me." It was an accusation of the Batista regime, describing its horrors and also outlining Fidel's plans for a new kind of government. To this day, it is worth reading.

Next, Fidel and his followers moved to a camp in the Mexican mountains, reorganizing and training themselves for another attack on the Batista regime. Fidel spent a lot of time traveling, speaking, and raising funds for guns and ammunition. The whole story was so weird; it could never have been invented. A young Argentinian doctor, Ernesto "Che" Guevara, joined Fidel in the mountains. He not only worked as a doctor, but proved himself to be an outstanding military leader.

When they considered themselves prepared, Fidel's little army bought a yacht called the *Granma*. They intended to sail around Cuba, land, infiltrate the Sierra Maestra Mountains, and form a foothold against Batista. Unfortunately, the overloaded yacht ran into engine problems; the sea was rough; and the men had to abandon the ship without their weapons. They managed to get to shore, and they spread out through the forest in different directions, expecting to meet each other on the top of Pico Turquino.

But Batista's military was waiting for them. Some were murdered, and others were caught and sent to prison. Only twelve of them, including Fidel, Fidel's brother Raul Castro, and the Argentinian physician, el Che Guevara, managed to meet at the top of the mountain. Standing on the peak, Fidel declared, "Batista, this is the beginning of the end."

Whenever I read this, I would shake my head in amazement: such optimism in such poor conditions.

With his dramatic determination, Fidel continued recruiting militants into his July 26 Movement, hiding, training, and growing in strength in the mountains. In 1958 the force was able to mount three strong offensive movements against Batista's police, and Batista was forced to flee the country. On January 1, 1959, Fidel's movement staged a triumphant march into Havana, where they took over the government.

The new Cuban government:

Fidel, with his charming, easygoing personality and good sense of humor, managed to enchant a good portion of the population. He promised to eliminate slums, provide free education and free medicine, and guarantee employment, and the people responded with overwhelming exuberance.

The promises sounded fine, but it came as a big shock to many when he really did start to carry them out. It wasn't long before the revolutionary government started taking over the foreign-owned private corporations, supposedly with some compensation.

The most controversial reform was the agrarian reform. Cuba's economy basically depended on the monoculture of sugar production. Most of the land, American owned, was simply confiscated. Local landowners were allowed to keep a thousand acres for themselves. Although Fidel promised to give each agricultural worker a parcel of land, it became more expedient to form cooperatives for the sugar crops.

With the stroke of a pen, everyone was given job security, including decent jobs for women in the "entertainment" (read: brothel) sector. After all, every industry could use more workers.

Everyone had the right to buy ownership of the house in which he or she was living. All education, even the university, suddenly was free. All medical treatment was free. The health workers, including the doctors, were to get salaries related to the type of job. All of these changes were helter-skelter. The government felt sure that they would make lots of profits from the nationalized industries. Fidel and his friends were compulsively idealistic, but did not have an impressive background in economics. (Today, I even wonder if our Western "top" economists know what they're doing.)

As the industries were nationalized, the previous owners socked away whatever money possible and fled to the United States, usually to Miami. On the other hand, people who had fled from Batista's bloody regime were now returning to Cuba as bilingual repatriados.

Of course, the Americans were stunned by the takeover, feared it, and hated it. In no time, they set up an economic blockade against Cuba, not allowing any American company to trade with Cuba and blackballing other countries from doing so. Canada was one of the only countries to ignore the blockade; Cuba always got its medications from Canada.

Seeing this, the Soviet Union decided it would be a good move to counter the United States by befriending Cuba, starting to buy Cuban sugar and giving it credit. Naturally, the world thought that Cuba was becoming part of the Soviet bloc. After a visit to the United Nations in December 1961, in a five-hour speech, Fidel Castro declared that Cuba was "neither capitalist nor Communist, but humanist." That was to change later.

After our supper that night, when my father announced that the mercenaries had invaded Cuba, I sat with him by the radio to get the rest of the news. Evidently Fidel was expecting the attack to happen and had made some preparations. The bombing on Fidel's air force actually hit dummy planes. When the mercenary boats landed in the Bay of Pigs, they were met by an opposing Cuban militia, and after a skirmish for two days, the invaders were all captured. A deal was made with President Kennedy, and the prisoners were returned to the United States, in exchange for money (which didn't all arrive.)

I make plans:

As in every teaching year, when school was out in June, my family spent two months in Vancouver, and in the summer of 1961, I was still taking university courses. One evening, a longtime friend of mine, Mary, invited me to go visit a friend of hers, who was just back in Canada for a while. I wasn't sure what to expect, but the new friend, Lisa, had spent a year in Cuba. Cuba was hiring as many specialized foreigners as possible, because a lot of their top technicians had left the country. Lisa's husband, a geologist, had a job helping the Cuban industry. All hired specialists were given spacious apartments and special privileges that allowed them to bring their families in comfort, which was the case in Lisa's household.

"Satya, why don't you visit us in Cuba? You could stay with us for a while," she invited.

Bing went my mind. It had never been a serious consideration before.

"I live in a lovely apartment building," she continued, "right on the sea, with a swimming pool, a grocery store on the first floor. We would love to have you." Oh, yes, and they had a maid! Lisa had a big family; I think I remembered twin girls and a grown boy, but she insisted that she had room for me.

The evening continued with her description of luxury in the tropics, while I started giving it some thought. I had spent nineteen years of my life considering how I could be useful in the world, and here was an opportunity to see what passionate young people were endeavoring to accomplish. I had never really wanted to see the Soviet countries, but Cubans were very different from eastern Europeans. They knew all about the American way of life, and they could not be hoodwinked. It was one thing to talk about how the world should change, but it was another matter to see how these efforts succeeded in real action. This was an opportunity to observe a unique social experiment.

"Yes," I replied, "I would like to see what was happening in Cuba." I was committed to working in Telegraph Creek that next year, but I could finish paying off my debts and save a bit of money. We made arrangements to visit Lisa in Cuba for the 1962 summer.

That winter, while teaching in the daytime, I spent the evenings intensively studying Spanish by correspondence. I had already done four years of French by correspondence. That meant lots of knowledge and no practice, but it was a good headstart. Lots of book knowledge does help.

As I learned more about what was happening in Cuba, I couldn't help but feel that the enthusiasm was contagious. Although I was taught to be cautious, I was excitedly optimistic about what I was to see. If there were mistakes, which couldn't be helped, we could learn from them, and march ahead. *Viva la Revolución!*

Three

A Very Different World

First steps in my travel:

June 1962, time for me to go to Cuba. Excitedly, I put on my crisp, new turquoise dress (that I had spent the dark winter nights sewing), grabbed my two suitcases, and, together with my parents, jumped into our large red Land Rover.

The first leg of the journey to the closest airport, to Watson Lake, was five hundred miles away from Telegraph Creek. The first one hundred miles of this route were on a one-way dirt road, fortunately not muddy, which wound along the edge of the mountains. At least we were able to enjoy all the reassuring pieces of greenery sprouting from the ground in the exuberant spring season. Finally we reached Dease Lake. There we met up with the state-of-the-art Alaska highway, still only covered with gravel, but with great curved banks that permitted higher speeds. This highway took us another three hundred miles to Fort St. John.

There in the Fort St. John airport, I finally was able to catch a larger airplane, which would take me Vancouver. My previous airplane experiences had only been in tiny bush planes. In Vancouver, I would transfer to a really big plane to carry me to Mexico City. My parents, excited and anxious, now leaving me to explore the big unknown world by myself, huddled over me as I climbed the airplane stairs. I remember the turquoise dress because Dad took lots of pictures on that stairway.

I start my journey to Cuba boarding a small plane at the Fort St. John airport.

Unfriendly Mexico:

As I left Vancouver, I had my first exciting experience flying on a large jet airplane which, in those days, served as
many delicious meals as possible. I finally arrived at the
bustling Mexico City airport, and I accosted a taxi to take
me to a luxury hotel. How had I managed to find the
most expensive hotel in Mexico? Having taken Spanish by
correspondence, I found that I could ask questions correctly, but I couldn't understand the rattled-off answers in
Spanish. The driver pulled out his bit of English, "Where
are you from?"

"Canada."

"Oh, what state is that in?" So much for literacy in
Mexico.

I spent the night in the hotel, as I was to continue
on the Cuban aircraft the next afternoon. During that
day, I decided to investigate downtown Mexico. So with
my purse clutched tightly against my chest, I ventured
out. I hadn't walked a block, and don't you think those
Mexicans were able to pickpocket me, extracting the wal-
let from my purse, without my noticing it. Not nice! My
money was in the form of traveler's checks (before they
invented credit cards), not much cash; but my driver's
license and cards were gone. Passport was okay. Here I
was in Mexico with no money.

When in distress, I knew to go to my embassy, so I hailed
a taxi. Fortunately I had not eliminated my name from
my parents' three-name bank account, so the embassy
was able to cash a check for me, but not until they had

billed me to phone for verification at the Canadian Bank ($15 then was like $150 now). Can you believe it, when I was in Cuba, eight months later, in the middle of the embargo and crisis, the traveler's checks were refunded to a Cuban bank in cash?

Now it was time to go to the Mexican airport. This was the final leg of the journey, and I was consumed with a mixed feeling of anticipation and anxiety. I was beginning to feel the excitement and optimism that I had seen in Cuban writings and reports from visitors; we were all convinced that, with passionate dedication, Cuba could try to change its world.

I searched the airplanes on the tarmac, and there it was! *LIBERTAD* was boldly written across the aircraft. My heart beat with excitement.

For the previous fifty years, Cuba had been dominated by American-financed yes-men, mostly bloody dictators, who took good care of Bacardi and Hershey, while the Cubans who did all the work lived in misery and poverty. Now, in two years, they had free medical, free education, and jobs. No wonder they felt like *LIBERTAD*. As a Canadian, I was helped onto the plane and treated like royalty.

Life of leisure:

Finally in Cuba, after the airplane rolled onto the steaming tarmac, when the door opened, I felt a blast of air so hot that I felt as if I'd put my head into an oven. In those days we had to descend a long, metal staircase and then walk through the heat. After all, it was July 2, 1962.

We scuttled across the boiling tarmac to the shade of the squat cement building. The simple little airport consisted of one open space with only a couple of immigration booths, all surrounded by a milling crowd of people who were laughing and shouting greetings. Everyone seemed happy. Interspersed in the crowd were a number of green-uniformed young soldiers, also talking and smiling, far from the regimented, stiff guards I had imagined.

Immigration officials were happy to see a Canadian and asked if I wanted my passport stamped. In the case of visiting Americans, Cuba didn't stamp the passports so that the American authorities wouldn't know that the traveler had visited Cuba.

I quickly found my friends, Lisa Gilligan and her family, waiting for me, and we exited to the airport parking lot. My friends drove me through the countryside's narrow highway, barely more than one lane, and although I had expected the sights, I marveled at the small thatched huts, palm trees, and even carts pulled by oxen and horses. No one seemed to be in any rush to go anywhere; the world seemed relaxed and even joyful. Closer to the city, the little one-story houses butted up against each other, but were usually painted different colors. Later we passed through the large lots with hidden glamorous homes—"the rich man's" territory.

The Gilligans drove to an underground garage underneath one of two brand new, luxurious four-story apartment buildings. Our building was called Edificio Riomar. I was taken to a west-facing third-story tiled apartment featuring every new amenity. I could imagine glorious sunsets from the balcony. Dishwashers hadn't been invented yet, but my friends had a live-in maid who had her own tiny room off the kitchen.

These luxury buildings, with their huge swimming pools, had been set aside by the Cuban government to house all the foreign technicians and professionals that they expected would come to help the Cubans. The tenants consisted of Russian families, a few Americans, a couple of Canadian families, and a select number of Cuban families. There was a foreigners' store on the first level where a privileged occupant could buy almost any food, even when there were scarcities everywhere else in Cuba.

Well, I wasn't really given a bedroom. I was to have a bed shared in a room with twin girls, and they had even invited another young woman to stay in the same room, so there were four of us. At least we had our own bathroom for the four of us. I was paying $300 a month for board and room, which was a lot in those days. They had a black maid, Maito, who lived in the tiny maid's room and who cleaned, cooked, and did all the housework. We were informed that we were supposed to pay extra and hire her to wash and iron our clothes (we were not given an option). Nonetheless, I was still pretty excited.

I was happy to rest in the sun and pools for a few days, where I met many other English-speaking foreigners. My first contact with Spanish was a funny incident.

An American lady, a smoker, asked, "Satya, will you run down to the little shop and buy me some matches."

Off I went, and in good Spanish, I asked for some matches. The answer was the most famous Cuban words I was to constantly hear, "*No hay.*" That meant, "There isn't any."

Testing my Spanish:

It wasn't long before I ventured off on my own. I was to meet a friend at a new commercial suburb on the waterfront, called La Rampa. To get there, I was to take a nearby bus. Naturally there was a long lineup, and a long wait at the bus stop. This was not a quiet lineup. Everyone at the bus stop was talking to everyone else, and they all looked at me. They immediately spotted me as a foreigner, and I guess I didn't really appear to be Russian. Someone in broken English asked where I was from, and when I said Canada, the whole group wanted to speak with me—in either English or Spanish. They asked me dozens of questions, but mostly they wanted to tell me about their wonderful revolution.

Life was going well at that time, particularly for people poor enough to ride buses. They all called themselves revolutionaries—and proud of it. Every one addressed each other as *companero* or *companera*." If you said that, they knew you were revolutionary too, and they loved it. There was no way a Cuban would use the word *comrade*.

Throughout all my years in Cuba, it was the custom that every person talked with every person. There was no way that one could stand side-by-side in a bus line, or on an elevator, and not be kindly enough to start a conversation. Talk, talk, talk, there was no such thing as a stranger. We were all humans, black and white and whatever.

Everyone and anyone spotted me as a foreigner (the blue eyes and looser clothing) and insisted on telling about "their revolution." My halting Spanish would trigger a torrent of one-sided Spanish conversation, and those who could, would drag out their little English, eager to try it out on me. The poorer people could not contain their great joy. Anything would be better than how they'd lived previously.

Young people, with nothing to lose, were the most active in social dynamics; they were still passionate that, with little effort, they could change the world. Older and middle-aged people looked on with interest, as it was obvious that this was uncharted territory. I guess the wealthier people were more shocked. Many had already left Cuba, but they still only rode in cars, so I guess I didn't have much opportunity to chat with them on the street corners.

Off to a new adventure:

After I had relaxed for a few days, I wanted to get going and do things. I wanted to see the country, to meet Cubans, to see different lifestyles. When I had been in Vancouver,

I convinced an obscure youth magazine to give me a press card, and I promised to send them articles, which I didn't have much intention of doing, but the card looked impressive and would be useful in opening doors.

On a nice sunny day, I walked by myself down G Avenue, to the Malecon, and entered an impressive new building, the Exterior Ministry. Overlooking the colorful harbor, it was made to impress foreigners about the seriousness of the new order and the revolution. At the entrance, the green-uniformed, proud young guard smiled openly, only too delighted to show a young foreigner the wonderful things the Cubans were accomplishing. We entered a cavernous, modern reception room, with its carved roof panels and windows.

"Good morning, *companera*. How can we help you?"

I showed him my shiny press card and told him I was interested in seeing what young people were doing in Cuba. "Just a minute," he replied and disappeared. Very soon he returned with another clean-shaven young man, elegantly dressed in suit and tie, who was secretary of something. Everyone in the hallways seemed so young. We sat down in the open, high-ceilinged lobby, surrounded by pots and pots of tropical plants.

"You are in luck. We have a busload of girls from a school of languages that will be leaving soon to pick coffee in Oriente [the most eastern province]. They are going as *trabajo voluntario* [volunteer work]. I am sure we could find you an English-speaking guide. You could go with them, and they will be leaving soon."

"What an excellent idea," I replied.

"You know, if you go, you have to work too. You have to climb mountains."

I smiled to myself. I was brought up in the Rocky Mountains, and to me the Cuban mountains were just foothills. Picking coffee couldn't be any worse than chopping wood. "Yes, I'd be glad to work."

Eagerly he leaned forward and announced, "We will supply you with the same gear that they have." The ministry chauffeur drove me in a Jeep to a downtown warehouse where I was supplied with two pairs of olive-green pants, two blue militia shirts, socks, underwear, and high black hiking boots. A real working outfit. It's a good thing that I also carried my own runners, as I found it a lot easier to climb hillsides in running shoes than with the stiff boots made for mud. I was all set.

Two days later, before the sun came up, and carrying my small suitcase of gear (no backpacks), I arrived by bus at the designated corner. A group of similarly dressed girls was already waiting, and I was introduced to Marina, who was studying English and was to be my companion. Her English was about the same as my Spanish—not very fluent. I didn't meet anyone else who spoke English, so I guess they were all beginners.

A rickety old school bus pulled up to the corner, and we all crammed in. The bus rattled across the narrow island highway, which felt just like the old Alaska highway—nothing new to me. During this trip, Marina narrated the whole story of what these girls had been doing the previous year, which had been called the Year of Literacy. These girls had lived in the countryside, in peasants' homes, and had taught everyone to read and write. When I returned to the city, in letters to my parents, I wrote about these girls' experiences, which I will describe a little later.

I'm with the girls picking coffee in the mountains.

We stopped at a thatched-roof, open-air cafeteria where our lunch was piled on aluminum trays. We ate black beans and rice, pulled pork, avocado, and *guarapo*—juice of freshly ground sugarcane. I was impressed with how tasty it all was. Even the traditional dessert, canned guava and cream cheese, was a great experience.

An old farmer peasant found out that I was Canadian, so he came to talk to me. "Who is the prime minister of Canada now?" he asked. He certainly was more educated than the Mexican taxi driver.

After about sixteen hours, we were dropped off at the end of the road. From there, we were to climb the hill trail for another three miles to get to the coffee plantation. The girls were worried about me and wanted to carry my suitcase, as they thought I was a city slicker and would not be able to make it. As it turned out, I scrambled up the hilly trail with the first three girls; the others were the slow city slickers.

We were lodged in a chicken coop, with hammocks slung from the poles. This was August, so the temperature was just perfect. This type of coffee grew on trees about twelve feet high, so we just pulled down the boughs as we gouged our shoes into the steep hillsides. Soon I was doing the more difficult terrains, as my runners were better than their boots.

The meals were cooked in big vats—usually rice, beans, and whatever they had slaughtered—and served on aluminum trays. I thought it was all delicious. After a week, I thanked them and, with my improving Spanish, returned to Havana in a public bus.

Marina's story :

This was Marina's story that she gave me in parts as we traveled in the noisy bus. From the first day of the new revolutionary government, it became a habit to name each year according to that year's goals. The year 1961 was named the Year of Literacy, since the majority of the Cubans, just as the majority of the Latin Americans, could not read or write. One of Fidel's priorities was to obtain a minimal education for everyone in the country.

In 1961, every student from grade six and upward was encouraged to spend the year on a farm or in a factory or small village where every night he or she would teach the farmers and laborers to read and write. Often, these students would work in the fields during the day and give classes in the evenings. Every "teacher" was given a kerosene lantern for the classes, as there was no electricity in many regions. I'm impressed how they managed it, but with this weak light, the farmers and their families gathered together with their teacher and, with pencil and paper, learned to read and write. Most of them reached about third-grade level that year, being able to read a newspaper and write basic letters. The following years, they would be offered classes to reach grade six.

This was an amazing feat, like pulling yourself up by the bootstraps. All of these girls had participated as teachers and were rewarded with *becas* (scholarships) to further their own education the next year. They were given free dormitories, clothing, food, vacations, and even a stipend for living. Eventually, free high schools were created in all their hometowns.

Up to that moment, and now even fifty years later, no Third World country has been able to emulate this effort.

The Third World is still dominated by children working in the sweatshops, with minimal classes.

Exciting job opportunity:

When I returned from Oriente, I continued to meet many different people. Unfortunately, they were almost all from the English-speaking community, which didn't help me to practice much Spanish. Many were English-speaking Cubans, repatriates who had returned from the United States. They became my first friends, and they took me all over Havana to see the sights, the world-famous ballet, and the museums. They were all thrilled with the changes taking place in Cuba and identified themselves as revolutionaries.

Jean, and her colleague, older than I, were two of my new friends. One day Jean asked me if I wanted a job. She had just heard about a two-month course that would be given so that we could teach English as a second language in the high schools. Since I was a qualified school-teacher, and I knew English, I was immediately accepted into the course. Jean and I got jobs in the same school, called Tarara.

Tarara was a has-been beach vacation community, about twenty minutes from the tunnel east of Havana. Most of the summer beach houses had been vacated, so they were converted into dormitories for students, and several groups of classrooms were constructed strategically. The dormitories supplied bedding, towels, laundry, meals, and transportation for the students. The young people all wore uniforms, which simplified the clothing selection. They had evening study groups in each of these comfortable houses, away from the city hubbub, and most went home for the weekends. Each house had about four to six bunks per spacious room, and everyone was cared for by a housemother-cook. Naturally, the boys had separate dormitories from the girls.

As in most parts of the world, the teenagers were more interested in each other than in distant facts and languages. I remember them as very polite, but not particularly excited about learning another language, even though they realized that English would be important in their future. However, I can say that they cooperated in class, but I just didn't feel that much sank into their brains.

As teachers, we were picked up by a bus in Havana, and we worked just one shift. I worked mornings, was given lunch, and then driven back to town. This way, I had the afternoons free. The paycheck, every two weeks, was in the form of an envelope with cash, and in all my seventeen years in Cuba, this was the form in which we were paid.

Under the gun:

One afternoon, when I returned to the apartment building Edifio Riomar, a strange incident occurred. For over a year, every now and then there would be sniper shots from little boats outside of Cuban territorial waters, probably from disgruntled exiles. Nothing serious had ever happened, and the Cuban Comite de Defensa (CDR) kept an eye on them. One day, while being closely observed by the CDR, one of these mercenary boats suddenly entered Cuban waters and started shooting—not little guns, but big mortar guns right at our buildings. Boom! Boom! Crash!

Frightened to death, the Russians in the building, who had just endured multiple wars, panicked and rushed to the lobby screaming. Fidel had to come personally to calm them down.

The Cubans, recently trained, calmly blocked themselves on the floor under the tables.

The stupid Americans, particularly a baker friend, having never faced danger, strolled out to the balcony to see what was going on. Later we found a huge five-inch hole on the cement wall, about two feet from where his head had been. Duh!

The Canadian slept right through it all.

Four

The October Crisis

Yankees are coming!

"Oh, my god, the Yankees are coming!"

October, 1962. I remember I was sitting in the glittery hotel ballroom, dripping with diamond-like chandeliers, which had been converted into a huge office. This was in the new, ritzy hotel, the Havana Libre (previously the Hilton) that towered over La Rampa, a new neighborhood on a hill with a glorious view of the boardwalk and the sea. Together with another group of enthusiastic young people, I was working on translations for an international sports medicine convention. Doctors had arrived from every part of the world, and they were strolling through the halls, laughing, discussing, and enjoying each other's company.

"The Yankees are coming!" Eduardo burst into the room. "I can see them on the horizon!"

"What?"

"Where?"

We all rushed to the north window, and there on the ocean, we were able to observe an American warship in the distance, cruising purposely just outside of Cuba's territorial waters. Not much later, another American warship followed.

The doctors were jolted. "What's going on? What right do they have to be there?"

We all had to find out what was happening.

The situation was explained to us that the American government had demanded that the Soviet leader, Khrushchev, had to get his missiles out of Cuba immediately, or the Americans would "not allow" the Soviet oil ships to enter Cuban harbors.

How were the Americans planning to prevent them? Were their warships going to ram the Russian boats? Or were they going to aim their missiles at the Russians and shoot them out of the water?

A large, important-looking British doctor bellowed, "That's impossible! That would be piracy! That's against international laws. That could be an act of war! The Americans wouldn't do that."

By the way, many of us wondered what missiles in Cuba did the Americans want to get rid of? The Cuban population didn't know anything about Soviet missiles. Besides, even if there were a Soviet base, who were the Americans to talk, since they had bases and missiles only a few miles from the Soviet border?

We (I now identified myself with the Cubans) were shocked, but not surprised. It hadn't been that long ago that CIA-supported mercenaries had tried to invade Cuba at the Bay of Pigs. It was also known that Fidel expected that they were planning another mercenary attack. Soon after that, Fidel had visited the Soviet Union, and Khrushchev, patting Fidel on the back, had promised him that he would always defend Cuba from any other attackers.

Gradually we realized that there would quite likely be a Soviet base on Cuban soil, but certainly not containing nuclear arms. President Kennedy challenged Khrushchev that the Soviets didn't have enough power to attack the United States, but the Russian replied that they could sure make a mess of New York.

I could just imagine the North American media magnifying every detail, fomenting as much fear as possible, in order to justify the continued arms race. Later I found out that it was called a "nuclear crisis," which created terror in the North American population. In Cuba, we didn't even dream that there would be an issue of nuclear use. Now, fifty years later, I came across the headlines in our *Vancouver Sun* newspaper, October 23, 1962: "US Blockades Cuba WE'RE OVER THE BRINK—Could Bring Nuclear War."

The Cubans were seething. Since when did Cuba have to obey what the big powers dictated to them? Cuba was an independent state, able to make its own decisions. Nevertheless, the rhetoric boomed back and forth between the Americans and the Soviets, each making ridiculous threats to each other.

All of Cuba's electricity depended on a Soviet ship bringing oil every fifty-two hours. The Russian ships were on their way, and the American warships hovered like vultures. Anxiously, we watched the detested American ships slithering past on the horizon, one soon after another.

The Russian oil ships were now getting closer to Cuba. People held their breath. If anything will unite a people more tightly, it's a threat from the outside. For or against Fidel, everyone was united in the desire to prevent invasion. Many in our translation group, as many other workers, joined the militia, where they were given uniforms and minimal military training. If necessary, these people would cover the whole irregular Cuban coastline in order to fight back any invaders.

The sports medicine convention was turned on its head. The doctors were appalled by the intensifying situation, and world politics became the main topic of conversation. Flights were canceled, and the delegates were confined to the hotel during the crisis. The atmosphere was strained, faces were glum. We didn't feel fear for ourselves, but there was fear about the uncertainty of the situation—that Cuba was completely isolated from the world.

Message from the outer world:

The second day of the crisis, our group was sitting around the luncheon table, and now many doctors stopped by to chat with us. In the middle of our busy discussions, a hotel administrator, arriving at our table, interrupted us.

"Is there a Satya Brown here?"

I raised my hand.

He strolled over to me, with a lumpy paper bag in his hand. "Satya, a package has arrived here for you—from Canada." He held out his hands and offered me the soft brown parcel.

What! A real package came through this barrier? Postmarked all the way from Canada? What was my mother thinking? Sending me clothes?

The whole room seemed to be alerted to this arrival, and many delegates crowded around our table to see me open it. After all, there was nothing to do but wait. I ripped open the paper.

What! A hoot of surprise erupted around us. I pulled out my old Chubby Checkers, a stuffed panda bear!

The tension broke, and everyone started laughing and cheering with relief. Here the teddy bear had managed to cross all the barriers; he had come to bring greetings from the rest of the world. Everyone wanted to hold the bear. He was carried all over the hotel, and many delegates' country badges were pinned on his chest. He became the mascot of hope.

There continued to be rhetoric between the Americans and the Soviets, and finally, as the Soviet boat was almost here, Khrushchev backed down and would take his missiles out. We were horrified. Khrushchev had promised help, and now he was backing out. Was it defeat? The truth was that there was never another attack on Cuba. So who won?

The next night Fidel spoke to the Cuban people—for five hours. Every radio in Cuba was on, with the whole population listening in silence. It was the first time that I was glued to the radio, and for the first time I was able to understand every word in Spanish. Fidel was upset and apologetic, feeling betrayed that this whole situation had played out without consulting Cuba once. There was some atmosphere of defeat, but we were happy to return to normal life.

Five

Family Expectations and Reality

Preparing for my family's arrival:

Now it was March 1963. I was still excited that Fidel was bringing my family to Cuba, and in the meantime I had been offered two jobs, so I was busy waiting. I was happily living with Lucila, and for once having regular meals.

"Satya!" I was called to Lucila's phone. "This is Vallejo. I'm coming in fifteen minutes. Let's get your house ready!"

I rode with Vallejo in his Jeep as he twisted and turned through little streets to the suburb with our chosen house.

I was absolutely delighted with our house. I just loved Cuban architecture.

Every house on the Calle Norte block was completely different—in height, size, distance from the street, and

Our house in Havana where I lived with my
parents after they arrived from Canada.

shape. I never tired of walking the block and snooping
at all the houses, like great works of art. Our house, the
squarest of all, was made of gray concrete blocks, so it
never needed paint. The roof was a gentle *V* shape, and
half of the house front consisted of floor-to-ceiling glass
window slats. Another wall of the front room consisted
completely of four wooden slat doors, and this whole
wall could open to what was now *our* side yard.

As I mentioned before, even though it was "open
concept," it had a separate galley-shaped kitchen, with
cleanable pink tiles covering two kitchen walls. These
houses in Nuevo Vedado were newly built in the 1950s,

so presented all of the comforts not included in the older houses of the wealthy.

Right away Vallejo sent me downtown to a group of three warehouses where they stored the furniture taken from the homes of the fleeing families. Every piece of furniture was piled helter-skelter on top of each other, making it difficult to distinguish what there was. I chose some beds, a simple kitchen table and chairs, bookshelves, and sofa and chairs for the front room.

We had now decided that Lucila would give up her house and live with us, living in our smallest bedroom with its own bathroom. We brought over any useful furniture from her place—her kitchenware, dishes, linens—and she and I moved in.

Lucila and I immediately had to sign up at the Food Ministry, where we were given our ration book, and we were appointed a store where we would buy all of our food items. There were a few *bodegas* in garages closer to us, but I chose a superstore about eight blocks away. The rations would be the same, no matter where we had to shop. I knew that my parents would be signed up at the foreigners' special store, with special rations, but it was far away, and I had no transportation. They would sign up when they arrived

Happy reunion:

"Hurry, hurry." Vallejo sent a message. "Your family is at the airport!"

I had not had any way to communicate with my family, so it took me by surprise that they were arriving. Immediately a chauffeur-driven Jeep arrived, I jumped in, and we rushed to the airport. After descending the long metal gangway, my whole family embraced me in hugs and kisses. The new adventure was so exciting; it felt like the old saying that "we could hardly contain ourselves." Soon we were home, where Lucila had everything organized and was cooking dinner.

A couple of weeks later, all the family belongings, including our red Renault Dauphine, arrived by ship through the Panama Canal. Now we were settled.

Vallejo dropped by two days later to make sure that everything was all right. In no time, Mum started requesting (demanding) a number of improvements that I hadn't thought of. She was sent to the same warehouses where she found a thick glass dining table that seated fourteen diners and weighed almost a ton. That was to be my table forever. No one could ever move it. She wanted an air conditioner for the master bedroom (thank heavens), and she wanted an enormous water-holding tank buried outside (thank heavens), and she wanted the carport roof turned into an enclosed patio opening from the master bedroom. No problem. All was done and delivered.

Not long afterward, a little pickup truck showed up, and a young man hoisted out a TV (the old ones weighed about two hundred pounds) and set it up in our living room. We were puzzled, but a note came with it:

"Compliments of Fidel Castro." That was the first TV we had ever owned.

My father, the invitee:

My father, Fred Brown, was the invitee, so he was the first to check out his proposed job. He had been hired as a philosophy professor at the University of Havana, even though, with Cuba's philosophical turmoil, the Department of Philosophy had not been set up yet. His first days consisted of visiting the university, meeting people, and anxiously studying all he could of Spanish.

In the third week, as we all sat around our monstrous table for supper, he began to tell us what he had discovered about this new department. As he ruminated, I had to watch the unlovely feet under the glass table. I hated the glass.

"It seems that they have chosen three of us to be the first professors of philosophy in Havana. There's me and a Cuban fellow who seems to have some kind of a degree in philosophy. Now they have a Russian guy who seems to like philosophy, and I guess he read Lenin in Russian, but he doesn't speak any English, and he's just learning Spanish like me. Right now we're having meetings about what could be put on the curriculum. Meetings and meetings and meetings. And can you imagine, I found out that there's no word in Spanish for *self-conscious*. How can we discuss modern philosophy without the self-conscious?" he went on.

He spent months on that word. Spanish had *timid* and *shy*, but the words did not have the same connotation. The meetings continued, the professors all received full pay, but no curriculum had been organized yet. A few months later, my dad took over the dinner conversation again.

"We're supposed to be now setting up the basic program, who will teach what. That crazy Russian announced that he was going to teach pragmatism!" Pragmatism was my father's specialty; he could quote just about anything in John Dewey's books.

"I mentioned to him that I didn't know that Dewey had been translated into Russian. It hadn't. The Russian was just going to pontificate on what someone had said about what someone else had written about John Dewey and pragmatism!" my father said.

So much for "learned professors." My father was beginning to feel that the whole issue was becoming a bad joke.

My parents spent a lot of time getting to know many other English-speaking foreigners, including Swedish, French, and other nationalities. They all hosted meals for each other and spent many evenings discussing current events. There was an endless list of issues: Cuban internal political turmoil, loyalties changing, men fired, others hired, ministries traded, and much more. Personally, I wasn't very aware of the details of the skulduggery, although at the time, I recognized the names.

By now, I was completely immersed in Cuban friendships and had little to do with the foreign groups. The
Cubans that I knew were still so passionately enthusiastic about their future that they felt these political events
were petty nonsense.

Foreign intrigue:

Among English-speaking foreigners, the members had
their own intrigues. Since Fidel had not really come out
and said what kind of a socialist he was yet, it was open
to all kinds of interpretation. He declared that he was
"Marxist-Leninist" and that he was getting help from the
Soviet Union, but Cuba was not yet considered part of
the Communist bloc. The first Canadian group to recognize Fidel and the Cuban Revolution was called the "Fair
Play for Cuba Committee." Well, horrors, the people who
ran that committee were Trotskyites!

Here I must digress to tell the story. After the First
World War, when the Russians managed to get rid of
their opulent monarchy, Lenin, a Marxist, became the
first prime minister. A number of adjacent countries
united with them, forming the first Communist state,
the Soviet Union. Their bible was short and sweet: the
Communist Manifesto, dedicated to the poor masses and
easily readable.

Lenin had two important disciples, or henchmen:
Stalin and Trotsky. When Lenin died (poor man's
corpse was on exhibit for fifty years), there was internal

bickering about who should be his successor. Stalin came into power, and Trotsky and his followers were exiled to Mexico. The two men had quite different interpretations of Marxist ideology and mutually hated each other, each claiming that the other had been duped.

Now what kind of Communism would Cuba have? Both groups were represented here to make sure that Cuba stayed on the "right" path. Historically, long before the revolution, Cuba had an insignificant pro-Soviet Stalinist Communist Party, led by Blas Rojas, that, at first, did not even identify itself with Fidel's government. They were not very influential. Thus it was anyone's guess: Stalinist? Trotskyite? Or something different?

In our household, many of the guests pushed different persuasions. There was staging, there were arguments, and some say there were even conspiracies planned. All wanted to influence Fidel, but I think that all they did was talk and try to bad-mouth each other to various influential leaders.

Personally, I didn't feel that the discussions were significant. The Cubans idolized Fidel because he wasn't going to be anyone's lackey, certainly not to old-time Russian Communism. All of these foreigners had a different concept of what Fidel was doing, right or wrong. The old fogeys could talk their hearts out, but the Cubans would go their own way. This brings me to introduce an elderly American couple, Maurice and Edith Halperin, Dad's best friends, because they became our best friends and would influence our lives forever.

Our friends the Halperins:

Multilingual economist Maurice Halperin, having worked as an American attaché in Latin America, having been ousted from professorship in Harvard, and having taught in France and the Soviet Union, had seen all the world's skulduggery firsthand. He had faced one disillusion after another. He and his wife, Edith, had moved to Mexico in the 1950s, and there met Che Guevara, who was part of Fidel's training group. Che told Halperin of their plans to take over the Cuban government, which subsequently took place, and Che immediately invited Halperin to be a guiding economist in the new government.

We met Halperin as he was still working in JUCEPLAN, Fidel's economic institute, and we knew that if anyone knew exactly what was happening, Halperin was in the confidence of everyone there. He saw every detail in the Cuban economy and the politics, the good and the mishaps, and he was able to analyze all the events from an informed outsider's view. Fortunately, he always saw events with a droll sense of humor. His wife, Edith, a mathematics teacher, looked like a hefty battalion leader. She had not bothered much with all the languages, but that didn't stop her from mangling them.

Involving the whole family:

My mother, Phyllis Brown, a very social, personable lady, excelled as the consummate hostess and Dad's partner in Cuba. She hosted many gracious evenings, involving big meals and long discussions. She could delve into many people's thoughts and activities. Interpreting personal and political nuances, she was a great aide to my father. She loved the swimming pools in the specified "foreigners' buildings," and every week a little Jeep picked her up to teach English to the minister Nunez Jimenez.

My sixteen-year-old sister, Heide, integrated into the landscape more easily than the adults. In Canada she had been studying high school by correspondence, so her first step in Cuba was to enroll in high school. Since I was teaching in the live-in beach high school, Tarara, she was accepted there and readily settled into a dormitory. I don't think she stayed in that school for many months, because she had heard of an opportunity to write an exam to enter directly into a premedical course. This had always been her dream, to be a doctor.

Last, but not least, my brother, Odell, with his family—Joanne and one-year-old Eddy—joined us in Cuba. They were immediately settled into a cute two-bedroom apartment, with a great balcony, about two blocks from our house. When I look back, Fidel's men sure took care of us. Odell was a mechanic and had a job working on heavy-duty machines. He wasted no time learning useful Spanish—truck-driver Spanish. Probably half their words were unprintable.

Odell drove his family around on a motorcycle, and one Sunday he noticed that the headlight wasn't working. The family was going to a barbecue, but he must remember to go home before dark.

They rode proudly on the motorcycle, what a stunning family they were, all cleaned up, best clothing, but, oops, dusk was falling. Stick to the little off-roads and hope that no one spotted them. Odell felt sure that they would, of course, be safe.

There in the dusk, a cop spotted them and stopped them. It probably didn't take long for him to realize that the family was not Cuban. In Spanish, the cop admonished, "You are driving this beautiful family without a headlight."

Odell had to think. For the life of him, he couldn't remember the Spanish word for broken.

"*La luz esta—jodida.*" ("The light is—fucked up.")

Imagine the shock for the poor cop, hearing this from such a clean-cut gentleman. Of course, he waved them on.

I imagine Odell's family had enough boredom, particularly for Joanne, who spoke no Spanish and couldn't even understand television. After a year, and after their daughter, Bonnie, was born, penniless they returned home, to flourish in their own culture.

Unintentional medical school:

I was teaching, busy, but not getting anywhere. I wanted to study political economy. I wanted to study sociology. I wanted to be a politician, in those days, when I naively thought that politicians had some say and some power in world events. In fact, I had still considered that road in life all the way up the eighties and nineties, until I was thoroughly disillusioned. To go into politics one had to be a "team player," which meant that one didn't dare have an original thought in one's head.

Thus I was antsy to start studying again, but somehow at the University of Havana, the faculty of political sciences still sat in limbo. They didn't know what teachers to use; they didn't even know what to teach. There was a Cuban Communist Party prior to the revolution, but it consisted basically of Stalinist old fogeys who didn't understand Fidel. That was the last thing we wanted.

My family had arrived, and we were living in our new house. My father was meeting other professors at the university and trying to learn Spanish. My sister, Heide, and my brother, Odell, were here. To tell the truth, I was bored, just teaching English in high school in the mornings and English in the Abraham school of languages in the evenings. My parents took care of the shopping and household chores, and as foreigners we even had special privileges, like housecleaners (they didn't call them maids anymore).

I wanted to get on with life, to study. All her life Heide had planned to study medicine, and I had once thought that I would pay her way through medical school. Just at that time, Cuba had intentions of producing more doctors, so they increased the enrollment in their very decent medical school. Many of the professors were Harvard graduates. As a way of increasing enrollment, they decided to have an entrance exam for mature students—people who had been away from school for a while or had not quite finished high school due to the revolution. Passing this entrance exam would qualify the student to begin an intensive premedical program.

Naturally Heide had heard about this and decided to sign up for the exam. I accompanied her. We arrived at the front entrance of the opulent eighteenth-century Havana University, which looked like an ancient Roman structure. The entrance was a wide grandiose staircase sided by pillars, reminding us of its majestic history. At the top of the stairs, columns announced the entrance to the different offices.

However, we were not to climb these wonderful stairs. We took a tiny sidewalk around the side of the building to a little rabbit-hole–like door at ground level. There we entered a small, paper-filled office where a kindly, aged gentleman smiled in delight to see Canadians. He immediately set about describing all the wonderful things that this medical school had to offer. Heide filled out the requisite forms and then had to return the next day with photographs of herself. I returned with her, and there she was, slotted to write the exam in three weeks' time.

The exam was primarily based on mathematics and Spanish (for Spanish-speaking people). Potential students had to be properly literate. Now Heide had her goal, but I went home feeling slightly jealous. I was still in limbo, doing nothing important fast. I continued to be bored, I wanted to study, I wanted to do something more active.

Then an idea began to percolate in my brain. I would sign up for the premed exam too. I could just follow in her footsteps. I wasn't really planning to be a doctor. I continued to muse, but a year of sciences would be useful for any career that I followed. I had studied a lot of physics and chemistry but had avoided biology. I was too afraid of having to dissect a frog in class. Ick! I hated blood and guts. However, I reasoned, if other people could do it, like nurses, maybe I could get used to it too. At least I would be studying.

So, for the heck of it, without breathing a word to anybody, I marched down to the little rabbit-hole office, got some photos, and signed up to take the premed exam. Done.

A couple of nights later, at the family dinner table, I confessed, "I signed up for the same exam as Heide. We can go together."

"What!" she screamed. "How dare you take a course with me."

"Why not?"

"Because you'll get higher marks than I will," she cried.

Everyone in the household was surprised but took it in stride. After all, one year of study did not mean that I was planning to be a doctor. We intended to return to Canada long before that.

Three weeks later, both Heide and I entered a large hall in the university, where about two thousand young people sat writing the entrance exam. The mathematics part was basically what we knew, but the Spanish part was different. We weren't very fluent at speaking Spanish yet, but we had studied the grammar carefully. Thus the exam, which in large part was about grammar, was actually quite easy for us. Heide and I had two of the highest scores in the whole group. We were now accepted in the course of premedicine.

All schooling was now free in Cuba, including room and board. Of the two thousand young people who applied, about two hundred fifty students passed the exam. Of those, about thirty students were chosen for an accelerated nine-month course; the others were to take two years for the program. Heide and I were in the first group, and we would begin studying in September that year. Now I really was excited to embark on a new adventure.

Six

The Disturbing Meeting

Early days in the premedical course:

N ow life began to rush by. The first week in September 1963, Heide and I were sent to another warehouse where we were supplied with two olive-green pleated skirts, two orange-trimmed gray tops, underwear, and black oxford shoes. We were to show up at the new school, designed especially for our small group, on Sunday morning.

Talk about luck, the premedical-school complex was only about a mile away from our house by the shortcut. The complex consisted of a grouping of empty upper-middle-class houses, perched on a north-facing hill, over-looking the river Almendares. Our gentle view consisted of a lovely meadow, then a little forest of huge leafy trees that accompanied the river through Nuevo Vedado to the sea. A block down the hill, into the meadow flats, a narrow one-mile road took us to the corner of our house. How convenient.

The school complex consisted of one larger home, where the basement was the kitchen and dining room, with all the spacious upstairs rooms set up as classrooms and offices. The other luxury homes became the dormitories for the students, with several bunkbeds in each room, where we lived during the week, and on the weekend we could walk home. The linens were supplied; the laundry was done for us; but how I hated ironing those pleated skirts. After school we did the minor household cleaning chores, and after washing supper dishes, the evening was dedicated to two hours of unsupervised study and homework.

Some students liked to study in groups while others studied on their own. The teachers had rotating evening visits to the dormitories, coming to answer any questions. Occasionally they would come in the afternoon for "inspection" that everything was functioning correctly, as, of course, it always was.

At first, Heide and I were located in the same house. For some unknown reason, I was designated "responsible," or the person in charge of the girls in the house, making sure that things ran smoothly, and I was the one who had to make the report.

One afternoon we were waiting for the inspection, peeking out the window.

"Oh, here he comes!"

And the girls rushed to tidy anything that was out of place.

As the inspector entered, I went to greet him. "Good day, Mr. Bocachula."

Instantly a swarm of girls surrounded me, nudged me, cutting me off from speaking. "No, Satya! No! No!" they exploded.

They had always called this teacher Bocachula, which I thought was his name. But it wasn't. *Bocachula* meant "funny mouth." His real name was Garcia. Talk about embarrassment. Hopefully he didn't hear me well.

It was assumed that we were all advanced students, so we were to learn everything at high speed. No more English. Our Spanish, which had started out as quite elementary, was being pushed fast. All of the classes—mathematics, physics, biology, and more—were all in Spanish. There were no textbooks, so it was up to the teachers, with the help of a blackboard, to explain every detail. We had to take notes on every little detail, because that was all we had for studying. Some professors were concise about giving good notes on the blackboard and explaining their topics clearly.

Heide and I were pretty good at taking notes. However, the biology teacher, a plump, pretty fortyish lady, spoke at the speed of a machine gun, occasionally writing illegible words on the blackboard, and although I was able to take notes, I always came out of that class with a headache. At the end of the semester, Heide and I got top marks in the exams, including biology. Whew!

Poor Heide:

Unfortunately, about three or four months into the course, Heide got ill and wasn't able to continue the course. She was diagnosed as having chronic hepatitis and was prescribed bed rest for six months. Knowing more now, I don't think that diagnosis was correct, but there I was, studying to be a doctor, and Heide wasn't.

During her months resting at home, now at the age of seventeen, she fell in love with one of my adult English students, resulting in a lovely wedding in our house. Her husband, Gerardo, was a young military man, but more as secret service (I think). He was stationed in the Soviet Union for one year, during which he was not allowed to communicate with anyone, particularly with any foreigner, so he and Heide had no contact for one whole year.

My brother and his family had just left Cuba, so Heide inherited his cute little apartment near our house. However, I believe she was very lonely. When after a year of silence, Gerardo was given a month's leave, with the possibility looming of being sent out again without contact, they decided that this was not a good basis for a marriage. They amicably divorced, and Heide returned by herself to Canada.

A dark cloud:

For all of my fellow students, the world was wonderful. They were passionate about the revolution that was giving them the opportunity to become doctors, all free, under the best conditions imaginable. In a sense, we were so busy studying, we were cut off from the rest of the world with no worries and no news. If there were problems, to us they were insignificant.

One day, a black cloud passed overhead. Our physics teacher was a tall, dark, and handsome young man, married to an equally beautiful physics teacher, both favorites with all the students. Always good-natured, sweet, and gentle, he dedicated his days and evenings to helping each and every one of us. We all adored him. One day, he didn't come to work. Then the next day he didn't come to work, and he never came back. After a short while, we heard that he had been put in jail for counter-revolutionary activities, possibly even a plot against Fidel. Plotting against Fidel's life was the only thing punishable by *paredon* (death sentence).

The feeling of misery and disbelief permeated our school. How could this be true? We were not supposed to have a cruel revolution. Were we to have *no* freedom of thought or speech? We knew that if we bashed the revolution out loud at work, we might be shunned. This world was not so perfect.

The beautiful day, the beautiful meeting:

One sunny Friday afternoon, the start of the weekend, I was relaxing, standing on the grassy sidewalk strip, enjoying the view of the meadow and the forest, when I heard a man's voice behind me, speaking in perfect American English. "How are you enjoying the course? What do you think of Cuba?"

There stood a nice-looking, smiling young man. Tipping his head slightly, his body swaying gently with his hand around a planted sapling, he continued a simple conversation. I, too, held on to another little sapling, enjoying the sun and nice conversation. I was enchanted. He knew who I was. I was the only person in the school with blue eyes, and everyone knew about the *canadiense.*

At the age of six, with his family, Luis Ramirez had gone from Cuba to Connecticut, where he was brought up, and then he had returned to Cuba a year after Castro's success. These repatriates, many of them middle class and educated, were bilingual and firm supporters of Fidel's attempts. He was now taking the same medical course that I was, and we would be in medical school together. We chatted for an amazing, relaxing half hour, until each of us was picked up for the weekend.

Throughout the following months, we often caught conversations with each other, ate in the cafeteria together, and eventually he walked me home, down the mile-long little road by the river. Then came the day that he walked me home and stayed. We were a couple.

Thus continued the life of the nine month premedical course. Final exams, and I was at the top. My Spanish was pretty fluent by then. They gave us a couple of weeks' vacation, then on to real medical school.

First years of medicine:

The first and second year of medicine consisted of all the basic sciences and medical sciences, so we still didn't have to work with live patients. This part of medical training was in a building complex called Giron.

In our first year of medicine, we were joined by many other students who had come from premedical classes by the normal route, and there were also a good number of students already in their second year of medicine. I've now, fifty years later, been asking my colleagues how many students there were in all. Each one guessed differently, so I would guess there were about six hundred students.

Giron was a large abandoned Catholic girls' school building on the outskirts of Havana. The two-story Spanish-style building, with its pretentious entrance, was a single story U-shape that surrounded a large open courtyard. The rooms were not adjoining; each one opened to a covered walkway that lined the courtyard. The previous year they had built four large amphitheaters, for lectures, each being able to hold at least two hundred students. The ground-floor classrooms were converted into multifunctional laboratories, each with the equipment necessary for its related subject.

Since the building was so far away from the suburbs, daily transportation was out of the question. We were housed in the empty homes—previous mansions of the rich and the famous. It was enlightening to see how the rich had lived. The servants' quarters were better than many people's homes. The bedrooms were huge, almost every one accompanied by marble bathrooms and every convenience, spacious living rooms, and humongous kitchens. Even the maids, cooks, and chauffeurs had their own quarters. As dormitories, the big bedrooms had about three double bunk beds, and we had comfortable sitting and studying rooms, often with the original furniture. The swimming pools were empty; upkeep was too luxurious for us. Many buildings had auxiliary power plants for the frequent power failures.

Linens were changed every week, and we continued with the pleated-skirt uniforms. Good thing they supplied irons and ironing boards.

I must recount an amusing situation. All of the Cubans rushed to have their baths in the few bathrooms, because they had to have their showers *before* they ate dinner. They ardently feared that if they got wet after supper, that might "cause a spasm" or whatever. I awaited the crazy rush and leisurely had the bathrooms to myself after supper. At first the girls were worried that "something" would happen to me, but they decided that maybe Canadians had some kind of built-in resistance to that "something." I was left in peace.

There was another incident after a couple of months into first year. Luis and I had been assigned to different groups, and he wanted us to be together. He presented himself to the dean, explaining how this poor Canadian girl, who might still have difficulty with Spanish, needed him to help her with her studies.

"Yes," replied the dean. "I have seen her exams."

I had just earned 100 percent on a histology exam, almost unheard of. Needless to say, we were not transferred together.

Every day we had classes in the amphitheaters, followed by laboratory classes in small groups. Textbooks were still at a premium, so we still had to depend almost completely on our notes. We had a new book in biochemistry, the latest and shiniest new American biochemistry textbook, but it was actually pretty useless. We had a huge old book in histology, reprinted with such a lousy press that we couldn't make out the pictures. Nobody cared about copyrights in Cuba—just copied and printed what was needed. Fortunately, we had good microscopes. I just had to memorize my extensive notes and not miss a thing. Our courses were still basic—microscopes, biochemistry, and lots of cadavers for anatomy. I finally had to get used to real anatomical practice, but it wasn't easy. Almost every doctor had one episode of fainting.

Not everything was good:

During this first semester, we experienced our first heart-wrenching incident.

Bleak! Despair. The moonlit night was dark, so very dark. Collective anger smoldered in our souls. This couldn't be happening, not in our beloved revolution that was dedicated to compassion and fairness for all its people. We were forty women living in this women's dormitory, a former luxury home. That evening we ate and did our chores in deafening silence, each alone with unanswerable questions and fears. That evening we had to attend a school assembly, a meeting that should never have been.

The ethical committee of our medical school, also known as a "student council," was dominated by very "revolutionary" young military people who had decided to become doctors. At this point in time, they concluded that the school should divest itself of some "undesirable elements." After all, we wouldn't want proven criminals to enjoy our free education.

Unfortunately, "undesirable" did not have a very fixed definition—hence it included counterrevolutionaries, people participating in the "black market," and even homosexuals. It seemed that it possibly could include any-body who had unwittingly participated in any so-called capitalistic endeavors such as selling a car or befriending someone who was secretly plotting evil. Anything could be stretched to look like "crooked" behavior. It was not a long list. Some of the people named were obviously crooked, but there were others who were our finest, and others with trumped-up charges.

We didn't dare complain, nor say a word, or we might be classified as a *gusano* too. Gusano meant *worm*, which was the expression used for nonrevolutionaries. One man on the list had just sold his car—a capitalist? Another one was the boyfriend of one of our girls. We loved him. He was the sweetest guy, but had he met the wrong friends? We were silent, and our hearts ached.

This process was called the *depuración*, which didn't sound too bad in Spanish, but translated into the horrible English word *purge*, it gave me shudders. To me, those words didn't have the same connotation; I preferred calling it "the purification." The truth was it was a purge.

Miserably we trudged down the dark trail to the school, each person silent with her own upsetting thoughts. The purge list was not necessarily complete. Who else could be on it? Would it be one of us? Did I complain about the revolution to the wrong person? Was one of my friends involved in counterrevolution, and might I be associated? Up until now, the atmosphere in Cuba had been easygoing, with folks spouting whatever criticisms they felt, but now they were examining our meaningless activities. How were personal activities being interpreted? By whom?

Silently we entered the large hollow auditorium and took our seats. No conversation. The silence was almost unheard of, particularly for Cubans.

On the stage was a long table where there sat a group of young men, our colleagues, many of them in the dark-green military uniforms.

The assembly began. The leader of the group explained their objectives, to only have honorable doctors. Then he read the first name, citing the person's previous "criminal activities."

"All those in favor of expelling him from Giron, please stand."

Silently the group of six hundred of us rose to its feet. The first few individuals were obvious criminals, or known cheaters, we didn't feel too badly. But then they mentioned a few people whose "bad" traits were rather dubious, and the group took longer to get to its feet. By now we were feeling even more uncomfortable. We were making a big mistake.

Finally they named the sweet young chap whose girl-friend was our dorm mate. We didn't even understand why he had been picked out, maybe some unwitting association with a "bad" element. Everyone in the auditorium felt horrified. How could we come to this?

Then the final question. "All those in favor of expelling him from Giron, please stand."

Nobody stood.

"Again, all those in favor of expelling him, please stand."

By now, these military leaders were glowering at the audience. Who would be next? Slowly, a few frightened people stood up, and little by little, the rest straggled up. I did not stand.

I was the only person still sitting. Of course, they could pretend that they didn't see me, or that I didn't exist. After all, I was Canadian.

It was a terrible event. No one talked about it, and no one mentioned it for several years. About ten years later, we all openly discussed that the purge *depuración* should never have happened. Interestingly, many of these "super military guys" did not perform very well on exams, and many dropped out before finishing medicine.

Several years later, we became good friends with one of these expelled guys. Luis Chansuolme, his wife, and many daughters lived in a tiny apartment, with the largest piece of furniture being a big piano. Luis didn't play the piano. He couldn't read music, but he was the composer of many of Cuba's most popular modern songs. He could hum or sing the tune, determine his desired rhythm, and then his wife would play it on the piano and write it down. He not only invented the songs, but he did all the instrumental arrangements.

When I asked him how he managed to write these songs without even reading the music, he replied, "It's like the ancient poets. Homer could neither read nor write, but he could recite the whole *Iliad*." Amen.

Seven

The Life-altering Decision

Big, big get-togethers:

Life in Cuba was filled with unconventional activities in which I participated at the beginning and throughout the seventeen years that I lived there. Here are a couple of examples.

In those early years, important events in revolutionary life were celebrated with immense gatherings in the Plaza de la *Revolución*. This plaza was a gigantic open space in the center of town, accessible from all of the neighborhoods (no urban sprawl here), surrounded by five four-story, gray cement-block government buildings and spaced out like a star. These buildings were ministries of this and that.

When the roads were closed off, the plaza offered an immense gathering place where a million people could mill around without getting crushed. There was a high podium at one side where Fidel could stand and pontificate about any important recent happenings, anniversaries, or new plans. He might be accompanied by some visiting big shots that he wanted to impress.

The foreigners walk into Havana's Plaza de la *Revolución* on May Day.

I remember on May Day, International Workers' Day, I joined our classmates in a little bus at five in the morning, and together with other medical students, we were dropped off at our designated corner. Dozens of groups, such as nurses, fishermen, or whatever, gathered on the streets. Then, group by group, they marched into the plaza. Some groups would walk in formation; many others just strolled along.

My parents joined the foreigners, who formed their own detachment. After everyone had arrived, Fidel, stroking his beard, would stand and commence his long, charismatic speech. He never read; he just started talking and then got more emotional, reaching a crescendo and reassuring everyone that the country was on the right track. If those Yankee imperialists would stop bothering us, our economy would be better, he said. Every speech finished with the crowd roaring *Patria o Muerte* (Fatherland or Death!)—a custom that started when Cuba was first attacked.

These gatherings were habitual on the three special holidays: July 26, the date when Fidel attacked the Batista fort in 1953 (which is considered the first day of the Cuban Revolution); January 1, when Fidel entered Havana and Batista fled; and of course, International Workers' Day. Other newsworthy events such as attacks were also justification for more gatherings. We carried our own containers of water, as there were no little kiosks selling things, although I vaguely remember little coffee bars on the outskirts of the plaza. We ate when we got home.

These activities were very well planned and well executed, and it was amazing what a large portion of the population participated. Only the disabled stayed home. I remember one July 26, I entered the plaza with a group from the south, and my sister, Heide, came in a bus from the north. In that horde of a million people, we actually ran into each other.

The crowds meet in the Plaza de la Revolutcion

As the years went by, the extra gatherings became less frequent, but the important three days were always celebrated. Once I had babies at home, it became difficult for me to attend, but I could always listen to Fidel on the radio.

Volunteer fun:

Another important activity of Cuban life was *trabajo voluntario* (volunteer work). Voluntary work was supposed to be a great privilege, a great honor. Since Cuba's workweek was five and a half days, that meant getting up early six times a week, and one extra morning, Sunday, which did not allow us any rest. However, it was made up by the joy of feeling useful and the enthusiastic camaraderie of being together with your friends.

Volunteer work was usually agricultural, or sometimes conducted in factories. Nobody wanted to do menial work, so dirty work was glorified. By 1962 the abundance left over from the previous economy was dwindling, and a shortage of labor was part of it. The seasonal workers who normally cut the sugarcane, and otherwise lived in abject poverty, had now found meaningful jobs in the cities or full-time work in the cooperative farms. That didn't allow for extra hands in the sugar harvest, so vast armies of people from other job sites had to be mobilized for these massive jobs.

In his long speeches, Fidel would praise the exemplary efforts of the Cuban people who, with the desire to improve the economy, marched forward to get the tasks accomplished at all costs. Nobody complained. It was a necessary part of life. For family people it was a nuisance, but there was nothing more rewarding than being involved in something useful. After all, this situation was to be temporary, until the economy got on its feet.

When it came to the big sugar harvest, from November to June, some men were taken out of their jobs for two or three months, lived in the country, and cut sugarcane all day. Each work center would have one or two full-time volunteers, so it wouldn't affect any particular industry. These people were rewarded with special privileges, such as being able to book beach vacations in the summer.

I had a funny adventure the first summer I was in Cuba. I had been with the young people in the Exterior Ministry. It was a young world.

"Satya, come cut sugarcane with us on Sunday!"

"Sure, of course."

"We're leaving at four in the morning, you have to be prepared to work hard!"

I rose to the challenge. With my new working clothing, I met the group by the road in the dark, and we traveled in the back of the open trucks.

We arrived at a real sugarcane field, with its long stalks of cane that looked something like bamboo. We were given machetes and sent to cut. I soon discovered that cutting cane wasn't that different from cutting wood with an ax—certainly an easy task from my years of homesteading in central British Columbia. So in a short time, I picked up a steady and easy rhythm. These *habaneros* were the true city slickers, so in no time I was at the top of their crew. I think between everyone's breaks, we may have cut cane for two hours. We had to be back to the trucks at twelve.

"Dios, you are very good at cutting cane!" the organizers declared, so they pinned some kind of gold medal on me. I have no idea where it came from or what it meant. Possibly some old military medal. They just wanted to impress me with their enthusiasm. So I had a medal.

For us students in Giron, we worked in the countryside four hours one Sunday a month, and occasionally, we had a whole month off classes in order to engage in more intensive harvests.

We had already risen early six times that week, so Sunday was another early morning. We dragged ourselves up at four, then drove to the meeting place closer to town where the trucks arrived, and all the volunteers were gathered milling around. It was still dark, maybe with a slight chill in the air, but an air of excitement. The fun of being together pervaded the atmosphere. Dressed in work clothes, we sat on the curbs, waiting for the final word that the trucks were ready.

Often, one hundred people would congregate in one area, and we would climb up the back of three-ton trucks with high sides. Many of us would sit on the floor, and others would stand and hang onto the sides of the trucks, and we'd ride away through the country in the quiet night, enjoying the rising morning sun. It actually didn't take long to get to the countryside, no urban sprawl here. The longest rides were one hour. The farther the better, I felt, more time in the truck and less time in the fields.

They'd drop us off in the fields, with lots of water jugs, and the local farmers showed us where we had to work. Sometimes we cut cane or weeded fields or picked tomatoes or dug potatoes. One hundred people can get a lot of work done in four hours. At noon the trucks were waiting to take us back to the city.

I remember one specific trip. They were building a new school, and it was time to do the landscaping. A large mound of soil had to be wheelbarrowed from the south side of the building to the north side of the building. So we pushed barrels until noon, with the job almost done.

Four weeks later we were returned to the same site. Unfortunately they had not considered who they were sending. The instructions were, "Please move this pile of dirt from the north side to the south side."

What? Wrong!

We were not going to move that dirt back to where it had come from.

We sat on the steps, where we chatted together until the trucks came four hours later. Let someone else move that dirt back.

My father is able to meet me:

At the end of the first year in Giron, we heard that there was to be an interschool debate on the topic of bio-chemistry. Interschool? Until then, I hadn't been aware that there were other medical schools in Cuba besides the one in Havana. There was a small medical school in Santa Clara, in the middle of Cuba. And another small one in Santiago, Oriente, at the eastern tip of the island. I was chosen to be one of the five delegates representing biochemistry from Havana. The debate was to take place in Santiago, at the other end of the country, and we were taken there in a big, creaky old school bus, sitting on hard metal seats for twenty hours on the bumpy old roads. I remember I spent the trip knitting—the only time I've ever knitted in my life, and the last time too.

Fortunately, on arrival, we were housed in gracious, comfortable dormitories.

More or less at the same time, Fidel was managing another activity. The first revolutionary medical school students had just graduated, and as a gift, he arranged that they climb the Pico Turquino Mountain, where Fidel had started the revolution. Of course these "mountains" were foothills to me. I came from the Rocky Mountains. It came to pass that my father was invited to join this large group of young people.

Pico Turquino was near Santiago, so after the climb, my father joined me there for the debate, and we had time together. I was slightly envious of the lucky group that was able to go to Pico Turquino. My father didn't tell me anything about it.

Fifty years later, as I read the biography of my father, Fred Brown, in the book by Van Andruss, *A Compass and a Chart: The Life of Fred Brown, Philosopher and Mountaineer*, I saw that Dad had described the trip of unprepared students in rain and misery as a trip through hell. So much for glorifying things.

The day of the debate, the participants all sat on the stage, and my father was in the audience. Each person was asked a specific question and was graded by his or her response. Lucky for me, they asked me a question that I had studied thoroughly. I had even made big charts on the topic. I visualized my chart and was able to talk forever. My father said that the professors behind me evidently threw up their arms as if "this was too much." I got a good score,

Fidel Castro with the medical graduates on a
special trip to Pico Turquino Mountain, where his
revolution started. Picture taken in 1963.

but best of all, by father was beaming with pride. I think
that was the best moment in medical school.

What road to take:

By now, both my sister and my brother had returned to
Canada. My parents were preparing to leave soon, too,
as my father realized that the philosophy here was not
as freethinking as he had hoped. Only slightly disappointed, he was on to new adventures in life.

As they were packing up, my father came to a gift that
I had given him on his arrival.

"Here, honey, I won't be taking this. I tried very hard to like him, but I just can't." It was a big marble desk set with a gold head of Lenin on it. That was that. Most Cubans didn't have a clue about what Lenin had written. I just remembered the phrase, "To each according to his need, from each according to their ability." Sounded good, but I was still in observation mode.

This brought up the question of *my* future plans. Would I leave with them, or would I stay in Cuba? Luis and I were very compatible. I was in love with him, but love was not completely blind. I knew that anyone I married, with whom I would have a family, would have to be someone who had my ideals and who could adjust to my two worlds. Luis fulfilled all of these parameters, so it was not difficult to decide to stay. We would soon get married. I wanted the wedding before my parents left, certainly nothing big and fancy, before the end of 1965.

"Do you want your parents' house?" Vallejo asked me.

"No," I answered. "Luis's family has a beautiful, big house with lots of room, and it would be convenient to be with my mother-in-law, Maria Teresa."

Thus, with all these plans in place, we entered the second year of Giron medical school.

Eight

Mishaps in my Cuban Wedding

Don't let the mishaps stop us.

The only wedding I had ever attended was my sister's wedding, a cheerful household party, but at least the whole family was there. Nonetheless, with minimal resources, we were to have a wedding.

Our wedding was planned for December 20, 1965. In the meantime, in between classes in Giron, I was fixing up our home-to-be, in Luis's house where he lived with his mother, and sister, Sofia, and husband, Fausto. It was an enormous, spacious Spanish home, the type that was built for the upper-middle-class in the twenties and thirties. It looked like a British set in the old black-and-white movies.

There were six of these similar tan stucco homes, looking like little castles that surrounded a circular courtyard patio. In the center sat a lovely, mosaic nonfunctioning fountain. The teeny tiny pieces of garden soil were adorned with big mango and citrus trees. Gorgeous.

Inside, the rooms were large, again the tan stucco and decorative trim, polished wood stairway, and floors of big black-and-white tiles. We basically had the upper story to ourselves with three bedrooms, two bathrooms, an open living room, and a gorgeous balcony. All of the rooms had glass windows that opened onto tiny wooden slats for air entry, and then the slats all pushed apart to allow the window to open wide. For our master bedroom, we chose the corner bedroom, which had windows on three sides, just off the balcony. It had a luxurious adjoining bathroom. It was an arduous job painting all those little wooden slats, without a thought of stripping the old paint or sanding the wood, but I did it myself. I considered myself lucky just to be able to obtain any paint.

Since the wedding was going to take place in the elegant front room, I wanted to have new covers for the old sofa. My mother was able to buy fabric in her foreigners' store, and an old lady was brought in to make it. I followed her step-by-step, as she held the pieces of fabric up to the sofa, cutting and sewing as she went along. That was the most useful class I ever had, as I now still make covers for all my furniture.

In the world of mishaps, our wedding would have won the prize. We didn't have a penny, so our friends the Halperins gave us forty dollars, enough to buy two gold, ill-fitting wedding bands. Other gifts totaled seventy-five dollars, enough for a three-day honeymoon, which we were planning to spend at a beach house.

The ceremony was in Luis's house, with his mother, his sister's family, my parents, and about ten classmates who weren't that close, but at least they were able to come. Somehow we had found some lawyer to officiate. Just as Luis and I were ready to descend the regal, polished stairway, which would be the "bridal procession," my dad realized that he had forgotten his camera, grabbed the car, and drove home to get it. We decided to wait a bit. We waited, we waited, but after a couple of hours, he still didn't return.

Finally we decided to carry on with the ceremony without my father and without pictures. We again descended the stairway, the lawyer said a few words, and we signed some papers. My new brother-in-law, Fausto, had donated a cake and some beer. I guess we had a few other edible items. The few guests quickly ate and then left. That was the total sum of the wedding.

For a honeymoon, we had planned to go to a hotel on the beach for a couple of nights, but now without the car there, that was not feasible.

Finally, my new father-in-law, Papa Louie, was able to rent us a room in a little hotel beside his house. The hotel was tiny, just a two-story wooden building, and our wooden room was painted green—everything: walls, closet, floor, bathroom—all green. I guess it was the only color in Cuba that year.

When we arrived at the hotel at midnight to sign in, the manager admonished, "A foreigner? You can't stay here unless you show us your passport."

Passport? It was at home, as I hadn't needed it for anything for two years. How was I supposed to go to my parents' house at midnight, no transportation, and come back for our wedding night? After a lot of fuss, the manager finally relented and let us spend the night.

Early in the morning, Papa Louie, who now lived next door, phoned to ask how we were! Doggone it! An hour later we got a knock on the door, coffee was being delivered from the next house. We dressed ourselves, took a bus downtown, and found a room in an affordable ancient hotel. We spent two nights on that main street downtown thoroughfare, bright commercial lights blinking in the window all night. We spent the day wandering around downtown. I remember I bought a tiny fuzzy toy bunny as a souvenir.

When we returned home, the first thing we did was ask about my father. He had decided to drive home on an unlit shortcut side street, and the car had rammed into an invisible high pile of gravel dumped in the middle of the road. It seems he bumped his head on the windshield (no seat belts in those days). He continued driving home, but it seemed he had had a concussion. He fell asleep in bed and awoke at 4:00 a.m., telling Mum, "Get up, we have to go to Satya's wedding."

Two days later, we returned to Luis's mother's house and took pictures of what the wedding probably had looked like. We were happy to start life in Maria Teresa's house; it would certainly help when there were children.

My parents left Cuba soon after the wedding. My parents' house was closed up, and I didn't think any more about it. When my father returned to Canada, he did land on his feet. He soon got a job as teaching in Behavioral Sciences, in the new liberal University of Simon Fraser in the Vancouver area. He also continued his experiments with intentional communities, with a healthy base of young university followers.

The beautiful Sofia, Luis's sister, and her husband, Fausto, were working full-time. When he had time, Fausto was a great cook. Nonetheless, there was no peace in the house. There was a lot of infighting among the three of them, even resulting in insulting language. Ma Teresa was left with the cooking, shopping, laundry and other chores, with no thanks, while the couple downstairs carried on with their chosen activities. Anyway, the atmosphere in the house was not as congenial as I had hoped, and even though we lived upstairs, we all used the same kitchen. It was making us nervous.

Again I thank Fidel for the house:

Back to Vallejo, I begged, "Do you still have my parents' house?"

"Ha, I knew you would want it. I have saved it for you. It is your home now. Here's the key." Very gratefully, we moved back into our old house, with the furniture still intact. I was in heaven.

The home ownership arrangement in Cuba at that time was that you paid 10 percent of your wages as mortgage for twenty years and then had ownership of the house. Since we were both students, we were not to pay anything. The world was not organized enough to charge property taxes. I don't know what kind of records there were of who was living where. I guess some people paid for electricity, but we never heard of it, and except for the frequent general blackouts, we always had water, sewer, garbage, and electricity.

Luxurious dormitory for married couples:

Now as a married couple, our situation changed in medical school at Giron. There was a specific house set aside for married couples that had about eight bedrooms. Since we came in the middle of the year, we didn't have priority, but we got one of the maids' rooms, which was ample, and a shared bathroom. I almost never saw the other couple. I remember it had the most beautiful bedspread, like a heavy velvet tapestry, designed like a purple and red oriental carpet.

The house had been built for the previous wealthy family. It was very modern, with spacious rooms, big garden, lots of windows, and the obligatory empty swimming pool. It was quiet, with lots of rooms and modern furniture where one could study. It was also only one block from school.

During this time there was some incident in the school that involved all the men's dormitories, so all the men in that course were punished, having to do forced labor for a month in a place called the Melba. This incident did not spill over to the married couple house, so Luis was one of the only men spared. To this day, our male colleagues identify themselves as the Course of the Melba.

Nine

Unimaginable Home Challenges

Unusual food shopping:

Thus we now began our married life in our own house. We spent the weekdays in the dormitory at Giron medical school, but we returned to our own sweet house on weekends. Now we had to come to grips with all the benefits and the problems of being homeowners. When our little Dauphine car was running, we could also drive home some weekday evenings, as it wasn't that far from Giron if one had transportation. All of the household articles such as bedding and kitchen utensils had been left in the house by my parents, so we could carry on daily living.

Now we faced the normal Cuban dilemmas of scarcities and survival, but we had no more foreigner privileges. Everyone in Cuba had to have a ration book in order to obtain food or dry goods. I had signed up a long time ago, but never thought much about getting food, as we were given three meals a day in our school. Even now in Giron, during the week we were fed, but we had to take care of ourselves on the weekends.

We signed Luis up in the same "supermarket" eight blocks away that I had chosen two years ago. Eight blocks is close with a car, but a long distance when one is carrying three heavy grocery bags. By the way, there was no such thing as grocery bags. One had to carry one's own bags, or simply no groceries. Since there were few cars for transport, there were grocery stores built into any building space every two blocks, which were often apartment building garages. It really didn't matter what store one had signed in as the rations were the same per person in every store in Cuba. In spite of that, when meat or vegetables came in, one had to get to the store quickly in order to get the choice cuts.

The food rationing had started two years before. All the basic staples were rationed: rice, cooking oil, salt, even sugar, meat, and beans. The amount varied depending on availability. The rice ration was two pounds per person per month, which the Cubans found very restrictive. They used to say, before the revolution, "He was so poor he couldn't eat rice; he could only eat *malanga* [taro]," which was considered baby food. Now they were complaining—where was the *malanga?*

The other staple was beans, which was rationed on availability, so a cook never could count on anything. I certainly learned to cook beans, and became famous for my red bean soup. The regular Cuban diet was always beans and rice, and hopefully pork; otherwise, they didn't know what to eat. Why they should eat rice, which was never even grown in Cuba, is a mystery to me. Potato harvest was from February through May, just an after-thought. Wheat was imported. White bread was baked every day, but one had to hurry before it ran out. This was not too good for working people; luckily there were often neighbors who would do the favor.

"Satya, Luis. The meat arrived at the store today!" Our neighbor would come running to notify us.

I would then say, "Luis, could you pick up the meat, and I don't think we've bought our rice ration yet, so get it." Hopefully we had a vehicle functioning at the moment, or it would be a heavy trip. "Don't forget to take the *libreta* [ration book]."

An hour later, Luis would return with our pound of meat (rationed at eight ounces per person per week, and later not even weekly, just when it happened to arrive). "I was lucky, there were tomatoes, and I was able to buy four tomatoes. I brought one tin of Russian stew, it was *por la libre.*"

We never went to a store "to buy something." We went to the store to see what was available and bought it whether we needed it or not, because who knew when it would show up again. *Libre* meant free, not free of charge, but free of the ration book.

Sometimes items were too abundant in Cuba. For example, at the end of the spring harvest season, sud-denly there were too many cabbages, or too many carrots, so you could buy as much as you wanted. They made a lot of sauerkraut, which was often available. One day there were too many cabbages, so they were piled in front of the stores with a sign "help yourself." There was no such thing as letting food rot in the fields. *Trabajo voluntario* would pick anything.

Frequently we had eggs *por la libre.* If there was no other protein, you could count on the chickens. Cubans were eating six eggs a day—two for breakfast, two for lunch, and two for supper. At the time I was doing my thesis on heart disease, but the eggs didn't affect the cholesterol levels of any of my patients.

Other items occasionally *por la libre,* like Russian stew, anyone could buy. I guess the Cubans didn't like it very much. Other times, canned sweetened papaya, which I loved to use for making "apple pie," was abundant and available. If I added orange juice and lemon juice to the papaya, no one could distinguish it from apple pie. From February through May was the fruit and vegetable harvest, so these salad foods were available but still rationed. I guess Cuba sent most of the vegetables to Canada.

There was one funny scarcity that made me laugh. Can you imagine rationing cigarettes? There were a few months when the cigarette ration was one package per week per adult. Of course, the nonsmokers gave their packages to the smokers, but the real smokers were in absolute misery. They smoked anything they could get their hands on. Any cigarette butt accidentally thrown on the street would automatically be surreptitiously picked up. They rolled the tobacco with any paper, even shiny catalogs. Remember, there was even a shortage of paper.

If it takes three butts to make a new cigarette, if you have nine butts, how many cigarettes could you roll?

Did you say three?

Wrong. After you'd smoked the three cigarettes, you had three more butts, so you could roll four cigarettes in all.

Uh-oh.

Dreary laundry;

As I walked out of the kitchen, I saw that the polished granite living room floor was covered with two inches of water! This was not the end of the world, because I could open the side wooden doors, which completely opened that side of the house, and just sweep the water out with a broom. But that took some time, and what a pain!

This was another big reality of life—laundry. The bottom line, all clothes were washed by hand. Outside, behind my modern house, were double highly polished granite laundry tubs, just a perfect depth and a perfect scrubbing surface, suitable for a high-class woman—like me. I would take the clothes outside, and with yellow, harsh naphtha soap, I would scrub. Sometimes my knuckles would get raw, and wringing heavy jeans out by hand was very tiring. Real whiteness was obtained by boiling the clothing in an aluminum bucket on the stove and letting it cool off. Then the clothes had to be rinsed, wrung out again, and hung up to dry. I was lucky, I had brought a pulley clothesline from Canada, which ran the length of the quarry space behind the house. I had to keep a close eye on things because items could get stolen.

For a while I had an old-fashioned wringer washer in the back of the house. Then we got really modern with an apartment-sized washing machine that fit in the downstairs bathroom. It washed the clothes—swish, swish—then we had to empty the water with a hose into the sink. The clincher was that we then had to fill it again with another hose, in order to rinse the clothes. I couldn't just stand there for five minutes waiting for it to refill. Time wasted when I could run off and do some other little chore. Sometimes, after a prolonged mental absence, I would realize that the water was spilling all over the granite floors—two inches of water all over the extensive living room. But even this wasn't the worse situation.

The demon of the laundry was our white doctors' jackets, of which we had two each. Almost every day these jackets had to be scrubbed, boiled, starched, and ironed. If it rained, I had to dry them in the house, and if they didn't dry in the high humidity, I had to get up at five in the morning to iron them dry. If I accidentally scorched them when ironing dry, I'd just sit down and cry.

Excellent quality laundry and dry cleaners did exist in Cuba; it was so nice to get the sheets and tablecloths perfectly cleaned and pressed. Those were the days when one had to iron sheets. What am I saying, I still do. Anyway, everything good has its price. I would walk the eight blocks uphill, hauling the dirty clothes in those wired metal-wheeled baskets (remember, no plastic bags), and join the large group of women standing outside the little laundry building. The laundry building was located on the triangular peninsula of a block across from the high cemetery wall, an area hemmed in by two busy streets that didn't quite intersect and buzzing with noisy oil-dripping buses.

"Who is last?" I'd establish myself in the lineup and then wait. Wait and wait, two hours was not unheard of. Some people just stood, most chatted with the others, some sat on their laundry. It was the world's greatest test of patience. No male would do this. Ten days later I would make the same lineup to pick up the clean things.

On one of my mother's many visits, she came to the laundry with me. She stuck her nose inside the building to investigate what was the holdup. She came back with the absolute answer, "I know! I watched them. They are on a slow-down strike!" No, Mother, no slow-down strike. That's just how they worked normally. It was becoming the story of Cuba. Why hurry?

What's hot water?

All of this brings me to a topic we take for granted—hot water. In fact, we were happy to have any water at all. For seventeen years I never had hot water out of a tap. Our house was built with a space for a hot water heater, but one was never installed. Dishes were washed in cold water, often with melted bars of facial soap since any other kind of soap was more than scarce. Clothes were washed in cold water. Baby diapers, all cloth of course, were boiled on top of the stove, then rinsed in cold water. For our baths, we boiled a little water on the stove, took it to the bathroom, topped it up with cold water, and then bathed ourselves with the bucket. One day I tipped the boiling water over on my feet. I was off work for a month. After that we brought an electric hot water kettle from Canada, which we boiled in the bathroom and dumped into our bucket. A real technology advance.

On one of my several trips to Canada, I ordered a real hot water tank from Sears, to be put on a boat leaving from Montreal. Just my luck, Sears refused to deliver it to any address that was not a residence. They would not deliver to the docks, so I never got my hot water tank. Cuba wasn't the only place with bureaucracy.

Here I am complaining about hot water, but in Cuba we were lucky to have any water at all. Frequently there would be no water for several hours at a time, and sometimes no water for several days. Many houses had tanks on the roof that automatically stored entering water, but this was barely enough to last for a day. In the case of days without street water, there would remain one functioning tap, usually a few blocks away, with a long line, and I could then fill one bucket. Imagine not flushing toilets for several days.

Thanks to my mother's insistence, Vallejo's workers had installed a huge underground cistern behind our house, which held enough water for a week. In a tiny padlocked closet behind the house was an electric pump that would shoot water up to our barrel on the roof. Even electric pumps break down, so the airport authorities were amused to see a big electric motor in one of our suitcases on one of our trips from Canada.

Short, miserable travelling:
Last, but not least, of the nuisances. A typical day.

I walked out of the hospital entrance, weary after working thirty-six hours nonstop. I stared longingly across the street to the bus stop. As usual, there were people roaming all over the area also waiting for the bus. I knew it would be a thirty-minute wait, just standing and hoping that I would be able to squeeze onto the next bus. I had to consider the alternative. I had to decide if I had the energy to walk home, which was up and down hill for half an hour, or wait for the bus for half an hour. Choosing the most reliable route, I started walking.

Transportation in the city was a huge problem. The last American cars were brought over in 1961, and Fidel had the only blue Chevy. Eventually all the American cars stopped functioning, so the government brought in Italian Fiats for government use and Czech Skodas for the few professionals. Soon we couldn't get parts for any of these vehicles, and all were confined to the graveyard. The best deal was when the government was able to bring in the Volkswagen beetle cars, which lasted forever, always had parts, and didn't use so much gasoline.

Most people depended on the public bus system, which could barely manage the huge numbers of new workers dependent on it. First we inherited the American buses, which lasted an amazing length of time, although they leaked oil all over every street in the city. As they died, buses came from Czechoslovakia (lasting one year), pickup trucks from Poland (one year), and hard-seated buses from Japan. Eventually Cuba was able to make a deal in the UK, and when I left, the Leyland buses were still struggling.

Luckily we had a car—some of the time. There were many times that it didn't work. We had brought a VW bug from Canada; otherwise, life might have been even more difficult.

Cuba did its best to devise ways to decrease the need for transportation. There was a definite emphasis on trying to get people to live near their work, or work near their homes. In our case, we were consigned to the nearest hospital—the smaller, modern Clinico Quirurgico, where we could walk in thirty minutes. Also, I loved that hospital, so we were in luck.

An interesting case was present the year I worked in primary care. In the middle of the residential area, there was a shoe factory, a two-story building that occupied a whole block. Since it didn't have an ugly parking lot, and it was surrounded by tall trees, it was not even visible.

Then the government constructed a number of three-story apartment buildings a block away, which were set aside for the workers in the shoe factory. Very nice.

No more dormitory living:

By the middle of 1966, we had finished our second year of medicine, and we were now finished living in Giron. We were now living permanently in our house. In the third year of medical training, we started hospital ward work and still attended lectures given in the hospital sites or at the central university.

By now I realized that I was pregnant. We had discussed when would be the best time to start a family. No matter when, there was no time that was "right." However there existed excellent day care facilities for babies six weeks up to school age. Should I interrupt classes, should I interrupt internship and residency, where my absence would be felt more acutely, or interrupt work in the countryside, where my work was indispensable? Since no time was good, heck, we decided to get on with it.

This third year we were first stationed in the military hospital, which wasn't really military. I had morning sickness, so I guess I didn't look very alert, which worried our chief professor. He didn't know my record, so he called us aside one day, recognizing that I might have difficulties with the language, and whatever, and offered any extra help we might need. He was very nice, and

Luis and I reassured him that we would be okay, and in no time he was pleasantly surprised. My first years in medicine I had managed to hover at the very top of the class, but after I had babies, I had to settle for just being good.

New problems—obtaining all necessary things for a baby. Right away friends donated a crib, some furniture, and some tiny baby clothes. However, I couldn't just go to any store and buy necessities. By this time in 1966, all the dry good stores were absolutely empty, with only the one or two items "available" that month, spread around on their shelves so they didn't look so miserable. I really didn't have the slightest idea of how to go about getting diapers, bottles, and such. Maybe there was a ration place for pregnant ladies, but we were not aware of it.

Besides, by now I was pretty homesick for Canada, so it was time for a visit home. My parents never had much money, but my father was now a professor at Simon Fraser University, so I knew they would come up with something. I was still very dependent on my parents, because Cuban money was worth zero outside of Cuba. I picked up a phone, which I did rarely, and asked my folks for round-trip tickets for me, Luis, and my mother-in-law, Ma Teresa.

At that time, the only way to get to Canada was to fly Cubana Airlines to Mexico, and then Canadian Pacific Airlines to Vancouver. However, paperwork was not that simple. It was difficult enough for Cubans to get passports and permission to leave Cuba, and even more difficult to get them visas into Canada. Again, Fidel's main helper, my dear friend Vallejo, stepped up to the young director in the Ministry of Foreign Affairs, with the order, "Take care of them."

We didn't realize how many and various things had to be "taken care of."

Ten

Misadventures of a Trip

Mexico specializes in making life difficult:

It felt almost surreal. Now December 1966. Luis, Maria Teresa, and I were all traveling to my home in Canada. I was now six months pregnant, and the bulge was beginning to show.

At last, after weeks of bureaucracy, Luis and his mother had their Cuban passports and their Canadian visas, and we had the tickets in our hands. The itinerary included using Cubana Airlines to Mexico City, where we would spend the night in a hostel, and then leave at 7:00 a.m. on Canadian Pacific Airlines to Vancouver. We were really on our way. I was so excited to be able to spend Christmas with my Canadian family, which I missed so much. I also planned to load up on certain items for the baby. There were so many things that were new to me and not available in Cuba at the moment. I had Spock's book on raising children—it was said to be the third most published book in the world, the first two being the bible and the *Communist Manifesto.*

The flight itself to Mexico was uneventful, back in the good old days when they gave you beautiful hot dinners on the airplanes. Cubana was the only airline that still gave out free alcohol, so it was a happy flight. We arrived at the Mexican airport about seven o'clock in the evening. We had very little cash (before the days of credit cards), so we planned to take a taxi to a youth hostel run by Quakers. When we passed through Mexican immigration, they looked at our passports and tickets, returned mine, but refused to give back Luis's and Ma Teresa's passports.

"You must pick up these passports directly from the ministry tomorrow at noon," announced the immigration official.

We were shocked!

"As you can see, we have a flight out at seven in the morning, and we need the passports before then," I replied.

"Sorry, you have to pick them up tomorrow at noon."

Well, we begged, we cajoled. The official called in another official, who also concluded that we had to pick them up the next day. We started complaining loudly, still stuck at that counter in the huge room filled with other officials and passengers milling around. We explained the situation to every official we could find, to no avail. After standing at the counter for an hour, we couldn't move until we signed a paper that we would pick up the passports at noon the next day. The Mexicans wouldn't return the Cuban passports.

We were confused and heartbroken. Those damn Mexicans did everything to make problems for Cubans! It was getting late; the airport was almost empty; and we were just standing in the now-empty lobby, not knowing what to do. At ten o'clock at night, completely stymied, we started wandering through the dark airport, along the empty, gloomy hallways. Eventually we came to a closed door where a sliver of light crept out at the bottom.

Amazingly, there was a tiny sign that read Canadian Pacific Airlines. We found the door unlocked, entered, and found ourselves in a warm, cozy little office, strewn with papers and daily paraphernalia. A coffee pot was brewing, but there wasn't a soul in the two small rooms. There we continued to stand, wondering what was next, when a short, mustached young Mexican man stepped in, "How can I help you?"

He was a staff member of the Canadian Pacific Airlines, so we spilled out our miserable story.

"Just wait here a minute. Take a seat and have some coffee," he said as he stepped out of the room.

A few minutes later he returned—the two missing passports in his hand.

"How did you manage to get those?" I exclaimed.

"They just wanted a bribe." Mexicans!

He went on to tell us, "There is a taxi downstairs waiting to take you to your hotel."

"Wait, we don't have enough money for a hotel. We are going to a hostel that might even be closed at this hour."

"No, Canadian Pacific will pay for your hotel. Go with the taxi. It will also pick you up at six in the morning, to bring you to your flight." There were no words to describe how thankful we were or how to thank him properly. I felt like hugging him, but he was happy to see us happy. "Anymore problems, just ask for Jesus Castro. Have a good trip."

The taxi took us to a luxurious hotel where we gaped in awe. We were given a spacious two-bedroom suite with a gleaming bathroom and all the amenities—things like soap and shampoo that we hadn't seen in ages. We were then led to a very fancy restaurant, with sky-high prices. We thought we would just order something small.

"Order anything you want," insisted the waiter, "anything at all. No money. Just sign the bill."

What wasn't I understanding?

"It's all on the airline company. Eat everything. Just sign." So we ate, so much that we almost got sick.

The next morning the taxi arrived, and we were given a warm welcome on the flight.

What they hadn't considered was that we had to change planes in Los Angeles, and neither of the Cubans had visas to enter the United States. Again we stood in the LA waiting room, confused at what we should do. Very soon a Latin driver showed up in a little electric golf cart. "Do you guys need something?"

We explained.

"Hop on." We did. He drove what seemed like miles, in the underground bowels of the airport, coming out in the corresponding waiting room miles away.

"Here you are. Wait for your plane. They will call you." We were on our way again, thanks to the Canadian Pacific.

We had a wonderful Christmas with the family. My mother-in-law, who couldn't understand any English, just sat on the sofa, cracking nuts all day. It hadn't occurred to me, but my dad thought we were coming up to stay, and we were bringing Ma Teresa as a babysitter. However, we studied the situation, and at the moment decided that our future was better in Cuba.

Same difficult Mexicans:

The return trip to Cuba was just as eventful. First, we realized that the Cuban passports needed visas just to pass through Mexico. As a Canadian, I had never needed a visa for Mexico. When our airline phoned Mexico, they were informed that the Mexican Ministry of Foreign Affairs, which issued the visas, was on Christmas holiday and would not reopen until January 15. Our flight was booked for January 3, and we had to get back to classes. No way. The Mexicans wouldn't budge.

I put in a long-distance call to our friends in high places in Cuba, which was not an easy feat. We explained our problem to get Mexican visas. The Canadian Pacific continued to harass Mexico, and I don't know if it got as far as ambassador to ambassador, but finally, the visas arrived on time. This time we traveled absolutely loaded, lots of overweight luggage, cloth baby diapers, bottles, nipples, clothing, soap, pens, toothpaste, and everything imaginable.

After an easy flight, we landed in Mexico and stayed at our planned hostel. Fortunately, we had a few days for a layover, because we found out that Luis and Maria Teresa couldn't return to Cuba without a reentry permit! Nobody had arranged these things beforehand. I guess they thought we wouldn't be returning. Again, with our last few dollars, we had the Cuban embassy in Mexico call the Ministry of Foreign Affairs in Cuba.

"Do everything they need! Quit giving them trouble!" were the orders from Cuba. Instantly, we were cared for and given first-class treatment home. But the buggers didn't return my phone money.

Eleven

The New Family

Baby comes between two classes.

Just a few days late, we arrived back in Cuba and were ready to start medical school again. I was very pregnant, but we were tucked into our cute little house with all the new goodies ready from Canada.

Now there was no more going to Giron. We were to have all our activities and classes in the hospitals, and at this point, clinical observation and even actual clinical work began. This was our introduction to real patients in real wards, where we were taught how to do physical exams and what they called differential diagnoses.

Luis and I drove our little red Renault car, fortunately still running, to the hospital every day. It was about five miles away.

We would start the day by attending the call change-over, which included doctors' reporting on everything that had happened of note the previous day. Thus we were immersed in every event, even though we didn't understand the topics yet. Afterward, we had one hour of lecture, followed by two hours of rounds. Together with the specialists, residents, interns, nurses, and other students, we visited every patient on our ward. I mean *all* the patients. They weren't given a choice (after all, they had free medicine).

At first we didn't understand much of what was said medically, but we were immersed and things were pointed out to us. Eventually we each had our own two or three patients, and we learned to do the complete physical examination as our job, and then we presented the daily follow-up to the group.

I think the best part of working in the hospitals was the loving friendships and relationships among all the workers in the hospital. I mean doctors, nurses, secretaries, cleaning people, patients—they all were constantly chatting with each other, interested in each other, maybe a little nosey, but actually caring for each other. They were such a heartwarming group of men and women, I just looked forward to going to work and being surrounded by such lovingness.

On Tuesday, February 23, I awoke at my usual time in the morning, ready to go to classes, when I realized that my underwear was moist. I didn't know much medicine yet, and I felt fine, but I wondered if this was a usual event during pregnancy. At least I was smart enough to think I had better check it out. We had a pathology class in the university where we should be going north, but my Marianao maternity hospital was to the south. Nevertheless, Luis drove me to the hospital. We would be a little late for classes. Going directly to emergency, since I didn't know anyone, and didn't know where else to go, I explained the situation to the attending nurse at the entrance desk. Soon an obstetrician arrived to check me out.

"I have a pathology class this morning, so I don't want to miss it, " I explained to him.

"You're not going anywhere. You're having a baby now," was the answer.

"What! I'm barely eight months pregnant!" I exclaimed.

"Well, he's on his way, so we'll be sending you to the birthing room pretty soon. His heartbeat is fine."

I was absolutely astonished, yet felt a little put out. I knew that babies could be born at eight months, but reality was a completely different situation. I lay on the stretcher, waiting, feeling fine, so I took out my microbiology notebook to study for the exam. Occasionally a nurse would come to check me out. I guess I didn't know it then, but they were checking how far I was dilated. At noon I started having cramps, then pain. At one o'clock I felt a sudden jab, like he was going to pop out, so I shouted. Just in time, the doctor and nurse arrived to catch the baby coming out. A boy! Hardly weighing in at five pounds, but he had an Apgar score of ten, which in med speak means perfect.

The baby started sucking and breastfeeding immediately, so in a few days, as soon as he started gaining weight, we went home. At the age of five months, this little Freddie weighed twenty pounds.

How sweet my three-month-old chubby baby was! He was sitting on my lap as we bounced along in a jam-packed rickety bus, early in the morning, going to the nursery school before I had to rush to classes.

Blub!

He looked up at me, gave me a beautiful smile, and then regurgitated his morning milk all over my clean green dress. Oh, no. I didn't have time to change or do anything. Here we were arriving at the nursery, then hurry, hurry.

Sometimes our car was working, and sometimes I depended on buses. In spite of these misadventures, I was lucky. The situation in Cuba was ideal for the working woman.

New rights for women:

Right from day one of Fidel's ventures, when he declared equality for everyone, it also meant equality for women. During the fight in the Sierra Maestra Mountains, a number of women participated—some of them with guns. I haven't really investigated, but I imagine they were the people who did most of the cooking, cleaning, and caring for the wounded. The most distinguished woman was Vilma Espin, who became the wife of Raul Castro. Once the revolutionary changes were in place, she became the minister in the Ministry for Women, an important part of government that had never existed previously.

Incidentally, Vilma and Raul Castro had two children the same age as ours, and they lived in a discreet penthouse a few blocks from our house. We knew if they were home or not, by the presence of a couple of guards outside.

In Cuba every woman had the right, and was encouraged, to get any kind of job she wished. Standard pay scales were set regardless of being a man or woman, usually depending on the amount of education the job required. In other words, a nurse would be paid the same as a plumber. Basic jobs, like cleaning hospitals, were shared by both men and women alike. Professionals had another pay scale, but all university graduates of different careers were all paid the same.

All working women had free childcare. I imagine that, when a baby was born, there might be a bit of a waiting list, but university students were given priority. The babies were accepted from the age of six weeks, and in many cases the grandmothers were the interim caregivers.

The *círculos*, or nurseries, were absolutely wonderful. The buildings were kept in perfect condition, and the well-groomed caregivers, dressed in pastel dresses and head scarves, were the most loving people imaginable. For the babies, one caregiver could attend up to six babies. However, this caregiver did not also have to cook, clean, wash clothes, or do any other housewife chore;

she was just there to play with the babies. Older children also enjoyed playing with and feeding the babies.

My son Freddie was first assigned to a nursery close to the university, which wasn't very near our home, and my classes were rarely in the university itself. Sometimes our car was functioning, and we were able to drive, but other times we had to rely on buses, which were always crowded and smelling of too many sweating, tired people. Not much later Freddie was placed in a nursery about eight blocks from our house, so we could walk, and when I had two children, I could push them both in the big old-fashioned buggy.

The best part was how much was encompassed in the care.

When I arrived with the kids in the morning, the first thing I did was take off their home clothing, store it in a locker, and dress them with nursery shorts and shirts. At the entrance of the nursery were little tables, usually with some new type of toy or activity, and the kids could hardly wait to change their clothes so that they could rush off and play. When I arrived in the evening to pick them up, they were clean, in their own street clothes, well-fed, and usually very happy.

Most of the nurseries were located in large empty houses or previous commercial buildings. All the rooms were painted in bright colors with children's paintings on the walls and little furniture built to scale. There were little troughs as sinks for washing their hands, and the taps had handles in the shape of cute, colorful animals.

A good portion of the toys imported in Cuba were allocated to the nurseries, but there were some very good locally made toys.

The children ate all their snacks and meals in the nursery, which might be scheduled to each parent's timetable, and I never heard of children complaining about the food. It was rice, beans, eggs, chicken, milk, and vegetables, and lots of crackers and bread. There was no junk food in Cuba. The children never had a choice nor were aware that anyone could have a choice of food. They ate what was available, no question.

Everything in the building was immaculately clean. The children even had baths or showers, as many homes didn't have hot water, and cleanliness was a priority in the nurseries.

Since both of my boys were premature, they didn't start day care until they were three months old, so my mother-in-law helped me out. Nevertheless, missing work or classes could be fairly routine and was perfectly accepted. At one point, my second son, five-year-old Carlos, had childcare in a previously private home at the end of our block, so he just had to run down there. Sometimes the little ones would take walks and pass by our house, and he would proudly show it off.

He loved the nursery, and he loved to eat. They told me that he would eat supper in the first shift, and then they would find him again in the second lineup. Of course, Cubans admired this healthy appetite. I must say, when food was scarce, it was good that they were getting some meals, and it made the rationed milk stretch for both of the boys.

Still superwomen:

This brings me to another part of a woman's life in Cuba. Of course, she could get a job, and maybe get house help from the grandmothers, but when she got home, the woman, not the man, was still the one who had to cook and wash and clean. A good man learned that he had to help out—maybe dry the dishes. The men were encouraged to help around the house, maybe take care of the kids while the woman did the dirty work.

Food shopping could be done by any member of the family. It wasn't as if the man could choose the wrong thing. At the grocery store one asked, "What do I have coming to me today?" and that bought everything possible. Rationed food was very cheap because prices were frozen at 1959 prices. However, even in Cuban pesos, we didn't always have a lot of money. I remember the first year back in the house, we had a small student stipend, and with our last nickel, I had to choose between buying the newspaper or picking up Freddie's chicken allowance.

If a child were too sick to go to school, it was expected that the mother be the one to stay home and care for him.

There was an episode when my husband and I both worked in the same nearby hospital, each in different fields. He was a surgeon, and I was an internist. One day, Freddie got sick, so I had to stay home. Luis went to work.

About an hour later, Luis returned from work.

"They sent me home to take care of Freddie. They said they needed you more than me."

I was chief of emergency at that time. Imagine what the male ego had to endure.

Endless study:

By now, I guessed that I might be a doctor after all, not just a passing bit of studying. It was like the cogs of a wheel, even though I never intended to finish medical school, once everything was going in that direction, life continued in that direction. Fourth and fifth years of medicine were primarily hands-on clinical work within the different specialties: ophthalmology, orthopedics, emergency, and others. By the time we graduated, we felt like confident doctors. In our last year, we were the real workhorses. We did all the work at the bottom levels and then reported to the superiors. We were not considered graduated MDs until we had finished our internships after five years of schooling, but we could intern in a specialty if we did not want a rotating internship.

From the third year onward, we had to be on call every three to six days. There were no pagers, and half of the students didn't have telephones, so that meant being on-site for thirty hours. We had rooms with bunk beds and proper bathrooms with showers, if there was time to use them. I just remember always being tired.

Carlos arrives:

When Freddie was one year old, I was pregnant again, and this time I was suffering constant nausea and vomiting the first three months. In fact, I lost thirty pounds in thirty days. Carlos was born at twenty-eight weeks of pregnancy, but he was in perfect condition—he just took a little while to learn to suck. He also weighed twenty pounds at five months of age. Quickly, the milk ration was not enough for him. I think that at two months of age, his molecular composition was composed entirely of yellow chickpeas and eggs.

Our new family, with babies Freddie and Carlos.

During my rotation of obstetrics, I was breastfeeding Carlos. On call, we students would take turns doing the deliveries. I always had the first turn because as soon as I finished, often at 3:00 a.m., I would rush out of the hospital, drive home in my little car, breastfeed the baby, and return to the delivery rooms. By the time I hit classes in the morning, my hand would keep taking notes, but my eyes would roll over, and the notes looked like squiggles made by chicken feet.

Somehow we survived and continued advancing in our studies.

Twelve

The Great Neighborhood

The Pilar Angel:

End of a shift, 2:00 p.m., and I was headed home, as I had been in the hospital working since 8:00 a.m. the previous morning. I had been on call the previous night and was lucky to have had almost four hours of sleep without being called. In the dead heat, I walked across the street to the bus stop and by some miracle was able to squeeze myself in the bus. As I clung to the pole in the bus, for the short ten-block ride, my mind was going over all the chores that awaited me—wash all the diapers, iron the jackets and school suits for the next day, check what food was in the house, decide what I would make for dinner, worry whether the water would be running, and wonder if there would be electricity this evening.

I pushed out of the bus through the people hanging onto the outside and walked down the three-block hill to my home. I entered and looked for the pail of dirty diapers. Empty. All the diapers were clean, dried, folded ono their shelf! What? The front room was dusted, the floor clean.

I knew that the angel mice, my neighbors, had come into the house and caught up on my housework. That was my neighborhood. This angel mouse had probably been Pilar. People rarely moved in Cuba.

Lovely static neighbourhood:

That meant that the people you know today would still be there seventeen years later. The houses just got fuller and fuller, as the generations added up. Our house was in the southern half of the horseshoe quarry, with a huge cliff towering over the backyard. Uphill to the north was a main drag, with buses and a movie theater, and in the other direction, downhill two blocks, was a beautiful treed park with a river running through it. This was Parque Almendares. My area had been a newer middle-class area, built in the fifties.

I loved this block so much for its interest and individuality. Each house was completely unique from the others, a combination of single-story, two-story, and even three-story apartments intermingling together. Some were set back, others close to the road, each with a different rooftop, form, and design. Every garden, or what would be a grouping of plants, was different. Plants just grew helter-skelter—bananas, bougainvillea, impatiens, palm trees, and others.

There was no planned format. The only "lawn" on the block was mine, but everything else grew graciously together. I never tired of walking the block.

The truth was that people didn't really have a backyard, just a little patio, large enough for a couple of chairs, a banana tree, and a chicken or rabbit coop.

The inhabitants of our side of the horseshoe, at least thirty families, all got to know each other over the years. We were not at home much, so socializing was minimal, but we always shared a word and a smile. On one side of our house stood a three-story concrete apartment building, each story with a separate apartment. The mother lived on the top, and underneath lived her son and family, which included two little girls the same age as my boys. We saw them when possible, but amazingly, due to everyone's busy work schedule, not very often.

Farther down was another four-story building, new and modern with lots of polished wood, glass, and balconies. Emelina lived in the center apartment, and she spent her life walking up and down the middle of the street, checking that all the inhabitants were all right, chatting and socializing with any person at home. To my surprise, when I returned to the block in 1990, Emelina was still walking the street, and miraculously I still remembered her name.

In front of our house, Ana, a university chemistry teacher, lived with her family. Their son Maito was the same age as my son Freddie, and Anita was the same age as Carlos, so they were all best friends, playing back and forth between each other's houses. We had a rubber wading pool (brought from Canada) on our lawn, which was where all the children on the block congregated.

One day Ana described how Anita and Carlos "played house" at her place where Anita had her dolls. When the "mother and father" went to bed in their pretend world, each one lay down with a big textbook to study at night. This is the concept they had of life while watching their professional parents!

My angel Pilar! She and her husband, Modesto, lived in a house at the end of the block. They were old enough to be my parents, and they became surrogate grandparents for all of us. Pilar took good care of us, often entering the house while we were working and leaving everything cleaned and shiny. Modesto could even fix broken furniture. They often cared for our children, and they frequently visited their house. I heard the cheeping of chickens from her backyard and, in the evening, the rattle of dominoes from their front doorstep.

On Carlos's seventh birthday, Uncle Julio, Luis' uncle, showed up with a huge white goose as a gift for him. What would a child do with a goose! I remember how Carlos sat outside on the brick border, with the placid goose, almost as big as he was, sitting in his lap.

"Would you like me to take care of your goose with my chickens?" Pilar offered.

Thankfully he agreed, so Pilar took him home, and Carlos went to visit the goose at her house. He went less and less frequently, until the time came that he never saw it. "Is it time to eat the goose?" asked Pilar. By then he understood, and understood food, so we did.

Naturally, if any neighbor got ill in the middle of the night, he or she would come to us and immediately get VIP treatment in the hospital. To be honest, even if a neighbor had gone directly to the hospital, he or she would have received the same immaculate care, but one always felt better if one's friends were standing by.

Over the years, Pilar did so much for my family that I didn't know how to repay her. Then one day, on a trip to Canada, I was given a functioning old television, which went to Cuba on a ship. Long before instant makeovers were popular on TV, we sent Pilar away for a day. We painted the walls. I reupholstered her furniture, added a few plants and gadgets, and ta-da, it was all new. It was the least I could do for them.

Carlos delights the ladies;

My younger son, Carlos, went to a nursery school at the end of the block, so he became sociable with all the neighbors. Then I heard that he would go to Ana's kitchen, sniff a bit, and say, "You are such a good cook. That smells delicious!" Of course the cook was flattered, so she would sit him down with a bowl of food. I felt that this was getting out of hand, so we explained to him that he couldn't eat in other houses since the food was rationed, and he might be taking someone else's food. We explained that to Pilar too.

The next evening the phone rang—for Carlos. It was Pilar calling. "Can Carlos come over to our house for supper tonight?" What could I say? The delighted five-year-old had an official invitation, so off he went.

Friendly watching:

Every time I returned to Canada, I kept hearing about how the Cubans had no freedom and that the revolutionary government was constantly monitoring and checking on citizens' activities. I guess they were referring to the CDR, the Committee for the Defense of the Revolution. The American press depicted it as a group of spies on each block who reported to their "higher powers" if some individual was out of line with the revolution.

This was really so far from the truth. I considered the CDR the same as the North Americans considered their neighborhood watch. They kept an eye out to prevent burglaries, rapes, or assaults, the same way they did in the North. Cubans could complain about the revolutionary system until doomsday, which wouldn't phase the neighbors, as many would even agree with the complaints. Generally, but not necessarily, everyone on the block belonged to the CDR.

Naturally if some house was collecting lots of arms, with the possibility of violence, that would be reported just as in our neighborhood watch. Members would take turns walking the streets off and on during a short shift, and it was a good chance to chat with the neighbors. No one carried guns, since most guns were collected after the active revolution. Some people had guns in their houses, and I remember once, when our house was burgled while we were sleeping, Uncle Julio gave us an old pistol to keep in our bedside drawer. Shortly, we returned it to him, thinking we were safer without it.

In all my years in Cuba, I knew many towns, and many, many people, and I never heard a complaint about the CDR. I suppose we belonged to the CDR too, but since, as doctors, we were on call frequently, we were never bothered with their schedule.

Cubans were naturally friendly and loved talking with each other. One could not stand in any lineup without a full conversation going on among strangers. In the neighborhood, everyone was checking to see if someone else might need help with a problem. This situation had a flip side. If they were constantly taking care of you, there wasn't that much privacy. If any old person didn't answer a knock on the door, soon an ambulance would be called. Since everyone conversed with everyone, it was difficult to keep secrets. Care for each other demanded knowledge of each other.

Pets still reign:

There were also the four-legged members of the neighborhood. You'd think that in countries where food was scarce, people would frown on having pets. To my knowledge, even the poorest countries had cats and dogs. In

Havana, a lot of people raised chickens or rabbits in their backyards, but these were hardly pets.

I felt it was essential that animals were part of our lives and that they could teach children not to be afraid. Animals could teach them the rhythms of life, so we had both a dog and a cat.

There were no such things as leashes or enclosed fences, so all the animals ran free. We had a yellow cat, Missu, and a medium-sized, short-haired black dog, naturally called Blackie. There were no such things as breeds, they were all mutts. Missu and Blackie knew that they were not allowed on the furniture and obeyed during the day, but in the morning they were lying on top of each other in the big chair. Thankfully, the chair was raggedy vinyl.

Blackie roamed the neighborhood. One day I found him lying on the floor in Ana's kitchen.

"What is he doing here?" I exclaimed. "Kick him out."

"No," she replied, "I love having a dog sometimes, without the responsibility, so I can send him home when it's time."

Blackie seemed to know that. He knew all the houses that were under his care.

One day a friend of ours, Pastor, who actually lived far away, was getting his gasoline at a gas station about ten blocks from our house. When Pastor went into the store to pay his bill, he had left the car door open. When he returned, there was Blackie in the passenger seat, waiting for a ride home.

At one time a chick had hatched in our medical laboratory (it was only supposed to be an embryo). Somehow, it survived, so I took it home and it slept on top of the dog. If it ran away, he would gently bring it back in his mouth. As is usually the case, pet stories abounded.

The (almost) paperless schools:
The primary school was a very important feature in the neighborhood. There was no question about one school being better than another. Children had to walk to school because there was no way they could count on school buses or other transportation.

The boys' school was a large one-story building that had previously been a private home and was now adapted for a complete school. I only went into the classroom once, but what had been a spacious bedroom was now a room crammed with little desks, with barely space for an aisle, with the requisite blackboards in the front. Most of the classrooms were similar.

The school was about seven blocks away, but first the children had to walk downhill into a gully, then up a steep hill for another couple of blocks. The building was on a flat space at the top of the hill, with enough space for play and games. I don't remember large patches of concrete, just soil, shrubs, and some trees.

During the rainy season, the rain always came after four in the afternoon, so, with the good drainage, their play area was always dry. Most of the time we dropped the children off on our way to work, which started at eight o'clock in the morning. The schools had childcare from early to late hours, even though the classes themselves were the standard five hours daily. For the kids who had to wait to go home, there were lots of activities, the favorite being baseball. Many times the children came home on their own, checked in at Pilar's house, and waited for us in the house. Freddie had the house key on a neck chain, and no one questioned the children's safety in the neighborhood.

The boys had to wear uniforms to school every day. Thank goodness they were cute. Two sets of long burgundy pants and pure white shirts were given to them free at the beginning of the year. If they dirtied them every day, it was a constant chore to keep them clean. Every kid had a little red bandana around his or her neck, and they got grubby easily. Privileged me, on one of my trips to Canada, I was able to buy burgundy cotton-polyester fabric that didn't require ironing, and I was able to make them two more easy-care outfits.

The one time I saw their classroom, I didn't see any books. I had to admire those teachers who could control all those students without books. They never brought a book home, and they never took a book back to school.

"How on earth did you learn to read without any books?" I asked.

"We learned everything on the blackboard, by copying everything."

That's hard to believe, but somehow they learned things. Somehow, they did reading, writing, arithmetic, and spelling, which was easy in phonetic Spanish. The school atmosphere was flooded with respect and tender loving care, and I figured that I was the one to teach them about the world. Children would occasionally get into fights, but I did not see prolonged teasing or bullying.

I did feel sorry that the boys did not have much of a chance to become readers. They mainly spoke Spanish, and there didn't seem to be any children's books in Spanish. I would read to them in little English books, but their comprehension in English was minimal. What time we had with the children was spent on life activities.

As everywhere, "believe what you are told":

Another issue nagged at my conscience while bringing up the children. They did not learn to question the world or think critically. If we wanted to be able to come and go from the country at will, we could not "rock the boat" teaching the young children to question the world around them. This was a priority to get them back to Canada at an early age—so they could realize that the world was full of people with different opinions and views.

Now they don't remember what it was like in Cuba. They just remember that they were happy, that they learned love and respect, and that they felt that they were "rich." I guess they were privileged, with their relationship with our Canadian family.

A few months ago, now in 2014, I decided to ask Freddie (now Fred) about his Cuban school life.

"It was wonderful!" was his first reaction, thirty-five years later.

"Did you have a shortage of pencils and paper?"

"Not in my school, we learned everything from copying things from the blackboard, and then answering the questions from the blackboard." He didn't remember any books because no one had books until grade seven.

"Those teachers were very good. They could teach everything intensively on the blackboard. We had sports, lots of singing, and dancing." I remember going to one event where Freddie did a Mexican dance, trying to dress like a Mexican.

"Did you notice any bullying there?" I asked him.

"Absolutely not. Every day it was drummed into our heads that everyone was equal on the whole earth, that every person in every form was to be respected. We even sang about that every day." (Cuba still had homophobia, but this was not mentioned nor understood at the primary school level, generally an issue kept silently in its closet.)

Carlos was not quite as enthusiastic about school. He was very hyperactive, always moving and talking, driving the teachers crazy. One time this hyperactivity was mentioned, and he was evaluated by a child psychiatrist. The result: "Yes, he is hyperactive. The teacher will be instructed to keep him very busy, he must empty the wastebaskets, sharpen the pencils, carry the messages, keep him doing physical things at all times."

In those situations the teachers would sometime rap the kid on the knuckles; now they give them a pill. It was just too much to hope to have twenty-five active kids in a tiny classroom behave like robots; each child had his own idea of how to react to the world.

Children dance:

In the 1970s, when disco dance began in the world, we heard the music on the radio. The international stars—ABBA, Bonnie M, Julio Iglesias—were played on the radio constantly, and the children loved to dance to it. On Sunday afternoons there was a television show for kids, *Para Bailar* (for dancing) with disco music for dancing, performed by children. Young and old loved the show and tried to imitate all its aspects.

The music was only available on the radio. There were no records or tapes for private houses. However, by then I was the proud owner of a ghetto blaster that not only played cassette tapes, but could also record on tape and be replayed. I would set up the tape machine in the kitchen and listen to the music while I was doing housework, ironing, or cooking. As soon as one of my favorite songs came on, I would run and push the record button, then push it off as soon as the song finished. After a couple of weeks, I had an hour's worth of disco music taped, so I suggested to the kids that they could make a *Para Bailar* party for the neighborhood children.

This was absolutely so exciting! There were no written invitations, but the word spread quickly to all the children. On a Sunday evening, with the furniture pushed back, the side of the house open onto the lovely lawn, and the big glass table set with snacks, the house started to fill with arriving children. Freddie and Carlos were dressed in their best, including white shirts. The little ones, also dressed to the hilt, and without parents, behaved like elegant, posh adults. Even the five-year-old little girl from the apartment of Los Muchos (maybe the poorest residents on the block) entered proudly with a long dress and a ribbon in her hair.

Then the music commenced. All the children quickly paired off and started to dance. The boys apparently asked the girls to dance. I say "apparently" because I didn't hear them, but observed what was happening. I didn't see anyone left out. I had explained to my boys how to be good hosts so that everyone could be included, but it was hardly necessary. The tape player blasted into the darker evening, all the little shadows dancing in our spacious marble-floored front room, and shadows of little couples dancing on the lawn between the shrubs. It was absolutely magnificent, and I felt proud that all of the children could have such a wonderful time.

Thirteen

The Peaceful Garden

Those critters:

Not all four-legged creatures in Cuba were friends. Plop!

A seven-pound lizard dropped onto my right shoulder! Then I shook him off, and I ran screaming back to the dormitory. This episode happened in the dormitory in Giron when I was taking the laundry off the clothesline under the lush trees. I never went back to those trees again.

My first awareness of the "outdoors" was when I lived with my parents. We particularly had lots of wild visitors if the side doors were open. The big lizard was a jungle aberration, not often seen inside the actual city. Small geckoes—called *lagartijas*—were a part of life in Cuba. First there were the tiny, delicate geckos with quivering red throats. They scooted around the greenery wherever there were a few plants. They had long tongues that flipped out to catch bugs, but they never came into the house, and they were harmless.

Then there were the flat, brown lizards scooting around the walls and the ceilings, and they lived in the house. I never saw them on the floors. Somehow, in our house, one of the lizards was nicknamed Mike. Thereafter they were all called Mikes. They chased the flies on the ceiling, but mostly we didn't see them. I guess they lived behind the big paintings hanging on the wall. Since they never came near us, we got used to the occasional sighting.

The worst creature was the humongous, light green, gelatinous gooey frog that could climb up any wall and come in a slatted window at night. They would always appear in the bathroom when you were half asleep. Lift the toilet lid, get ready to sit down, and the evil green eyes would be staring at you from the toilet bowl. Imagine it jumping on your bare ass. Or if you just wanted to wash your hands, there he was in the sink, ready to jump on your face. I'd scream, and my dad would come get rid of them. As time went by and we acquired dogs and cats, we saw fewer frogs in our house.

Garden sanity:

For me, fun in the sun really meant life in a garden. I had never had a garden at my young age, but I remembered the garden our family had inherited (but not gardened) in a tiny house in California when I was eight years old.

I never saw a tool. I never saw anyone gardening. The plants were just there. The pathway beside the house was lined with calla lilies, and there was a plum tree in the middle of the yard with real plums.

My grandmother taught me to snap the snapdragons, and how to suck the honey from the honeysuckles. By the front entrance stairway, where I sat with my little girl-friends, there was a big geranium bush on each side. The neighbors had flowers with funny faces—pansies. Seven-year-old memories are funny.

I had always had a hidden desire to have a garden, and now, for the first time, I had a house. Vallejo had encouraged me to help myself to the empty neighboring lot, so in deference to the other neighbor, I helped myself to half of it.

The cliff behind the house and garden.
Notice how the front wall opens.

I knew nothing about soil, land, or fertilizer. I just vaguely knew that plants needed a bit of dirt and maybe occasional water. Our house was situated, literally, in a quarry, and behind there was a three-story precipice that had another road and more housing at the top. Our garden consisted of an adjacent vacant lot, situated to the side of our house, where, luckily, the four wooden side doors to our living room opened to this space. It consisted mostly of gravel with just a hint of nutritive soil.

I decided it was only fair to share the vacant lot with the neighbor, so I made a line up the middle of the lot, from the street to the cliff, where I dug up a garden border, planting along the street and up my "line." All the time I was at that house, I kept the border planted with a row of different plants at different times: first it was lined with hibiscus, then with coffee plants, and then with oleanders. Closer to the house I occasionally dug up little patches of "dirt" and tried to grow other things, usually unsuccessfully. The front of the house had a tiny patch of lawn and canna lilies previously landscaped, which just stayed that way for years.

I wasn't aware that there were such things as garden shops where one could buy tools, fertilizer, and bedding plants. Maybe they didn't exist in Cuba. But come to think of it now, I did pass some kind of garden shop on the way downtown, but I was always too busy or not curious enough to check it out.

Luis's Uncle Julio showed up with half a dozen banana sports. The back of our house had been the beginning site of a new high rise, so what remained was rubble and pieces of rebar. The baby bananas were tucked between the rocks, with only a hint of soil, and they thrived, each one not only producing a batch of bananas the first year, but also five or six more saplings. These new babies also produced their own bundle of bananas within one year, so harvest season was at least one bundle a month all year long.

Our first bunch of bananas grown in craggy
soil in our backyard in Cuba.

Eventually I harvested about thirty bundles a year, half of them sweet bananas, and the other half cooking bananas, called plantains. The sweet bananas were smaller and sweeter than those imported in North America, but they weren't the dwarf ones. There were as many as two hundred little sweet bananas in each bundle. The cooking bananas could be cooked green or ripe, with an extended list of recipes. Yum. Bananas grow so easily in frost-free areas, in any soil or gravel, with little water, that they are always in season. It is said the bananas are the largest weed in the world. Great!

Portioning my side garden in the shape of a rectangle, I eventually got chain link fence from Canada, and I planted shrubs in a row along the perimeter. My first border consisted of a line of Mar Pacifico (red hibiscus), which, with very little water, seemed to thrive in these conditions. Then one year there was pressure to grow free coffee bushes, so out came the Mar Pacifico and in went about sixteen coffee plants. They grew. I picked the coffee beans. The next step was to put them out on the deck to dry in the sun, although it could rain. Finally, after months of "drying," I gave them to my friend Pilar to roast and to grind. It all made just one pound of coffee—just not worth the effort. Out came the coffee, and I remember the last time, I planted rows of oleander.

A sour orange tree probably came from Uncle Julio, and it thrived too. To this day, I miss sour oranges so much. They were the perfect marinade for red meat. The world is missing something that was common for the Cubans. I took the seeds out of a ripe papaya, dried them, and planted them in a little pot. Soon I had lots of seedlings transplanted and growing well on my rocky hill. I learned that half were male, that didn't produce fruit, with only half being fruit-bearing females.

The first year I was in the house, a neighbor was pruning his poinsettia shrub, from which he handed me a big stick. I shoved it in front of my big picture window, and amazingly it grew and bloomed. They grow into four-foot-tall shrubs, and they bloom from November till May. Absolutely stunning! I inherited a big group of orange canna lilies, which were always in bloom in front of the large window. With no fertilizer and little water, I was convinced that anything could grow anywhere. When I brought back pansy and petunia seeds from Canada, of course they didn't show their heads. Strangely, the Canadian radish seeds immediately grew into huge radishes.

What I missed was a lawn, which one rarely saw in Cuba. One day Uncle Julio arrived with a gunnysack full of little chunks of sod, so I dreamed of a luxuriant lawn surrounded by flowers. I dug each little chunk into the ground, about four inches apart, pushing them into the sand, grit, and gravel. I watered and watered and I waited and waited. After two or three years, the little pieces finally seemed to grow together. We were the only people with a lawn of any sort, so I was happy. My mother brought a series of rubber playing pools for the boys, so our garden was the center for many of the nearby children. It was great!

Children play in our yard in Cuba.

With a lawn, we needed a mower, but there was no such thing. I did find a gardener. I traded him two pounds of rice to mow the lawn, which he did with an old push mower. He also cleaned up the plant area with a long-handled edger that, to this day, this gardener taught me howto use that edger to weed and keep my garden clean with minimal effort.

Fourteen

Fun in the Sun

Happiness is a sunny beach:

How many people can you fit in a Volkswagen bug? In the years 1959 to 1964, that was a well-known challenge—and also somewhat of a joke. Young people would try to break the record of how many people they could squeeze into every inch of the tiny car. For us, it was how many family members we could take on free Sunday. Most weekends were usually blocked by work call schedules or a broken car or bad weather. That meant that we had a good beach trip only occasionally.

We owned a beautiful, shiny red Volkswagen bug that came all the way from Vancouver, Canada. We had decided that the only make of car to bring to Cuba was a Volkswagen, as it was the only vehicle still importing parts. Thus on one of our trips to Canada, we were able to buy a cheap VW bug. The little red car started its magnificent journey (just like Mozart's journey) in Vancouver. It took the ferry ride across the strait to Vancouver Island, drove to Port Alberni on the Pacific Coast. There it sat for six months until it was finally loaded on top of a ship eventually destined for Cuba. The ship sailed through the Panama Canal, stopping at all kinds of exotic ports, and finally arrived in Havana.

After some complicated paperwork, and giving up our rotting Renault, we had this marvelous little red car in our carport. We certainly were among the rich and the privileged.

How many people could we take to the beach? The VW had a little pocket behind the backseat where we could actually squeeze in four small children. Then two adults could bend over and sit on the laps of two others in the backseat, plus two people in front. That was ten. In the front space, we stowed blankets, towels, food, and all the beach gear. Several times a year this was the height of fun.

Bacuranao was a wonderful little beach about twenty minutes from Havana. It was a small, sandy beach, hidden behind some pine trees and hidden from the tourists. The children could play in the sand, and, later, Luis took the boys out on the water with goggles, snorkels, and even spear guns, where they could spend hours at a time. I think the kids learned to swim before they even learned to walk. I dunked them in the water in a little lifesaver when they were just five months old. During these beach trips, it was my turn to curl up in the shade and, marvelously, do nothing. If I was lucky enough to have a book, I might be reading.

Freddie and Carlos at the Bacuranao beach in Cuba, 1974.

When I returned to Cuba in 1990, I searched for Bacuranao and couldn't find it. The beach was just a blip on the coast because all of the pine trees had been removed. Rafael, the medical colleague and friend who had spent a year in our house, told me that they had taken down the pines for "ecological reasons." Huh? Yes, the pine trees were turning the sand into dirt. I thought to myself, could that be bad?

The other big beach adventures were longer stays in beach cabins, usually shared with other families. The most coveted beach trip was a chance to stay in Varadero, which actually happened fairly often. These cabins consisted of abandoned luxury beach homes of the rich and were used by the tourists during the winter. However, in the summer the luxury cabins were available for Cubans, so we usually fit in one family per bedroom, and we shared the other facilities. Since money wasn't really an issue, and every person in Cuba wanted to stay in a beach house, we had to be on a list or have a winning friend invite us. This happened maybe every other year, and it was pure heaven. Sometimes we had to take our own linens, food, and toilet paper, and usually we had the guarantee of having running water!

Occasionally we were lucky enough to stay in hotels, and a number of times we were able to stay on the great beach Varadero!

An excellent source of entertainment was the movies that were shown in ornate, scrumptiously old-fashioned red-carpeted theaters. We had one of the best theaters within walking distance of the house. Cuba unashamedly pirated the very best colored movies from every country, and the prices were cheap and available for everyone. However, the Cubans were quite good at making their own comedies. We saw only the very best of the American, French, British, and Italian movies. I guess they were carefully selected, so we thought that these countries made only good movies. The Russian movies and Polish movies were not only boring, but managed to have all the heroes die. With everyone dead, the show would be over. There were movies suitable for children, with real-life bears and squirrels in nature documentaries. I loved it.

First years of that new invention-television:

Great efforts were made to import enough Russian televisions for the whole country. On our fuzzy black-and-white TV, the only kind in those days, we could see all of the old American and English movies made in the forties and fifties, with all the old stars—Humphrey Bogart, Errol Flynn, Barbara Stanwyck, and we could also see the equally brainless old Argentinian movies. The Hungarians and Czechs were able to make gentle comedies. On TV, the subtitles were unreadable, so I only watched the English-speaking movies. I don't know how he did it, but my son Freddie could watch the crazy Russian movies for hours.

The largest park:

Besides the beach, the enormous Parque Lenin park was the site of occasional entertainment. It presented many acres of natural, open palm-treed Cuban countryside, with lanes winding all through it. The little road was dotted with about eleven kiosks where people could drop in without a ration book and buy goodies not available in other places. We could buy little chocolate bars, packages of cream cheese, little yogurts, and ice cream. Naturally, we bought as many as possible, then bought more at the next kiosk. What we purchased was limited only by how large a refrigerator we had. There was bus service to the park, but you really had to have a car, or a friend with a car, to get about, but it was a great treat.

The park had an outdoor amphitheater carved into a hillside, with rows of comfortable seats carved in stone and grass, just like the old Roman forums. At the bottom there was a small lake with a big stage floating on it. Most of the time, the lake was kept empty, but was filled when there was an event. I remember going to a show with a Mexican dance group, and there were some men who danced on the tip of high telephone-type poles. What a spectacle!

One time my mother brought us a kite from Canada that was blown up and shaped like a pillowcase and painted with a huge Canadian flag with the red maple leaf. The ideal place to fly it was Parque Lenin—the best venue for wide open spaces. There we found a large empty field, we blew up the kite flag, attached a rag tail, and hooked a string of heavy-duty fishing line. Let's see if it could fly.

It was a windy day, so we ran, pulling the string, and up the huge kite leaped to the sky. We were excited to see our Canadian flag flying high in the air, when suddenly—SNAP—the string broke and the flag was loose. It started to descend slowly, but in the meantime, it weaved all over the place. We chased it, wanting to be in the area when it eventually landed. As we ran, we noticed that the flag was headed for the narrow park road and heading straight toward a car. The car had to stop; then more cars had to stop. The drivers stared in amazement at this monstrosity bounding toward them, with us running behind on the road! It was so funny, we took lots of pictures with that lousy 35mm German slide film that faded in two years. That kite never flew again, but it was enough. We had great photographs of the flying kite, but the German film faded to nothing over the years.

Our marvelous, and only party:

"Where do we put the ice?" announced Alfonso, holding a gunnysack dripping with huge chunks of melting ice. We were having a party. By some miracle, a group of us third-year medical students had decided to have a real party, and naturally it would be in our house. To have a party, it was necessary to have beer and music. One person in our group knew a little band that set themselves up with a small loud speaker in the middle of our living room.

All of the guys cooperated. They filled the upstairs pink bathtub with ice. They arrived carrying a dozen of those old wooden crates filled with tall brown bottles of beer, and the band arrived. We opened the whole side of the house onto the lawn, put a tablecloth on the huge glass table, and set out the beer.

Ah, I thought, we must have snacks with beer, which were not easy to come by. About thirty or forty friends had arrived. I cut down a bunch of cooking bananas from a banana tree in the backyard and made fried tostones with them. Delightful! But the party continued, more noise, more beer. So one tree at a time, the guests went to the dark back of the house and cut down more banana bunches. I think I must have fried about thirty-five large green bananas. It did the job though. I said it was a miracle because that was the only party I ever saw in Cuba.

We had a house party with friends from medical school.

Otherwise, all Cuban parties were based on family get-togethers, often large enough and mostly related to someone's birthday. Birthday parties for children were actually quite elaborate with the three generations of family, and every child on the block was invited (without their parents).

Child's birthday party in Cuba.

Every now and then, someone in the family would get ahold of a ham or a sheep or a pig, and we all celebrated, almost always in our own open-concept house where the kids and everyone could spread out. Also, beans were a Cuban specialty, and for some unknown reason, I became famous for my beans.

Children pull the piñata full of candy.

One time I wanted to "entertain," as shown in the glossy American magazines. I carefully, personally, invited four couples for a dinner, specifying the day, time, and place (our house). They understood the invitation and were delighted. That evening I set the table beautifully for fourteen, had everything cooked, then waited for the guests. We waited, we waited, we waited. At nine o'clock that night (dinner had been planned for seven), we realized that no one was coming. They all had transportation, but no one phoned, nor later mentioned it. It was just not part of their concept; I guess they just didn't understand. That type of formal entertainment was not part of their culture.

Welcoming foreign visitors:

Our greatest joy came from visitors from out of the country. The most frequent visitor was my mother, who was now divorced. She showed up at our doorstep for a few weeks at least every year. She always came loaded with lots of extra bags in her hands. She would find fellow travelers who didn't have handbags and ask them to carry her bags on. Cuban mail was notoriously slow, sometimes taking several months, so every time someone came or went, visitors would carry letters both directions. I always sent Mum a list of things I needed, and she would bring them down, and much more.

I think every year I asked for lightbulbs for my Christmas tree and cherry flavoring for my fruitcakes. She would always bring shampoo, pens, and books, and on her own she would decide to bring some good clothing from the Salvation Army, which we could wear, remake, or "sell." I am eternally grateful for the unusual fabrics she would carry, enough so that I could redecorate the house. I certainly was spoiled. She was a fantastic shopper.

We always had a bedroom for Mum and welcomed her. While we were at work, she had a lot of Cuban friends (mainly boyfriends) who would pick her up and entertain her constantly. Other times she was a great help taking care of the kids.

I remember one Sunday morning, we were enjoying the beautiful morning with the whole side of the house open onto the garden. Two little boys, not from our neighborhood, came shyly to the edge of the garden and looked over at the house. In a friendly way, my mother came out and started talking to them, in English, of course.

I heard the little boys quietly speak to each other. "That lady doesn't know how to talk." Then they disappeared.

Of course, Cuba had its share of foreigners, including Canadians, but they seemed to live in a different world. Sometimes we would dine at some diplomat's or technician's house, followed by a few visits, but besides that we had nothing in common. These North Americans were often in Cuba for short stays only.

Canadian nostalgia:

Did I think of Canada? I remember an episode when I was working in the hospital. I was strolling from one ward to another, passing through the large common room that always had the TV on, when I suddenly heard the strains of "O Canada." I stopped right then and there. The television was showing Pierre Trudeau, then the Canadian prime minister, with his wife, Margaret, and a tiny baby, perched on top of the stairway exiting the airplane in Havana. Right there, in front of all the relaxing patients, I burst into tears. My beloved, tall black professor was passing by too, and he came and put his arm around me, patting me on the back.

"There, there, our little Canadian doctor. Of course you miss your homeland."

The Cubans never questioned my sentimentality; they were just glad to have me for a while.

Of course we attended the big reception at the Canadian embassy for Trudeau, with all the Cuban and foreign dignitaries present. Margaret sought me out and handed me a letter that Mum had sent with her. We also attended several other Canadian embassy receptions, usually on the first of July. Once CBC radio interviewed me about how Canadians abroad celebrated the first of July.

During my seventeen-year stay in Cuba, we returned home for vacations a number of times (I've never counted them). Unfortunately my parents had to pay for most of the trips, but we were able to pay for one boat trip in local money. We only passed through Mexico on that first described trip. Otherwise we had to go by ship from Havana to New Brunswick or Montreal, or wherever. Then we had to cross the continent by train, at least four times, and eventually by airplane. Most of the time, Luis came with us, but sometimes I went alone with the children. The first time my grandmother paid for a flight, we sat in the new, massive 747 airplane. It felt like a huge theater, and I felt that it could never get off the ground.

When we went by train, we sometimes had a little private room, and once by myself, we had one Pullman bed, and the kids traveled and ate free. They could order anything and everything that they wanted in the dining car, and they loved talking with all the fellow travelers. Carlos, age one, raced up and down the aisles in his walker, getting lots of attention. When the train arrived at the Atlantic side of the continent, we transferred to a large Greek ship carrying powdered milk to Cuba.

I remember several ships. One was a smaller ship carrying cattle to Montreal, and we had our own little room. On that trip the veterinarian shyly came over to me.

"I have a couple of sick cows. What dose of penicillin do you think I should give them?" Asking me? I was just a doctor.

"I guess twenty units should do it." How did I know?

Another time we had a large, luxurious private room in a Greek ship carrying powdered milk to Oriente, Cuba. We weren't allowed in the control room, but the sailors carried the children everywhere and gave them all kinds of little presents. The Greek servants knocked on our door several times a day, insisting on bringing us little cups of lousy Turkish coffee (lousy to us because it wasn't strong enough).

Eventually airlines were able to fly to and from Montreal, so we were able to travel by air. These planes, even the Canadian ones, were not allowed to fly over US airspace, so they had to go over the Atlantic. In the final lap of our trips, as our airplane hovered over Vancouver, my eyes always watered. No matter what, Vancouver was always "home."

These trips home were real periods of relaxation for us. Sometimes we stayed with my parents and grandmother, and sometimes we stayed at my brother's house. In Canada our Cuban peso was not even worth a cent, so we were completely at our family's mercy. It probably wasn't easy for them, but they certainly made us comfortable. At that time my father was a professor of behavioral sciences at Simon Fraser University, and my brother, who owned his automatic transmission shop, also flew little airplanes. Our boys certainly experienced the variety of activities that existed outside of Cuba.

Fifteen

Topsy-Turvy Economy

How scarcity affects survival:

What is economy anyway? I used to think that some experts juggled a whole bunch of numbers around to come up with a number called GDP, which somehow meant "growth." It certainly didn't mean growth of my paycheck. I imagine that if the GDP (or gross domestic product) went down, then a business owner might worry about not having enough sales, and if the GDP went up, an unemployed person might have hopes that he or she could find a job that year. Maybe. I don't think it made much difference in my life.

Who would ever know what the GDP was like in Cuba in 1958? How did Cuba stand in "economy" language? At that time Cuba was considered a Third World country. That meant that there were rich owners of a number of industries; there was an upstart middle class; and there were new roads, bridges, and modern homes being built in the cities.

The big centers and the owners of farms and businesses now had electricity, and some had telephones. I was lucky to have a telephone in Cuba. Not all of the middle class were yet part of the creeping telephone service. The majority of the population consisted of either unemployed, poor working people, or peasants who worked on the farms. Most of these people lived in hovels, could neither read or write, nor had access to any medical services. This is the group that Fidel Castro and his cohorts promised to give a better life. I don't think they were considering any GDP. They promised equality for all, education for all, and medical services for all. That was a big, unheard of promise.

Just imagine the situation that Fidel and his friends faced in the mid-1950s. Their objective was to get rid of the horrific, bloodthirsty tyrant Batista, with the idyllic vision of making life better for everyone, including the huge poor population. Although Fidel was trained as a lawyer, thank heavens, since he had led the revolutionary movement since 1952, he had a little background in leadership. His first challenge was to convince the population to support him. In this, no one doubts that he was a great politician. Second, his organizers had to have the military knowledge to conquer an organized army. There is no doubt that this was accomplished. This alone captured my imagination and also made an impression in the rest of the world. The details of this military feat are explained in the 1960 book *Cuba: Anatomy of a Revolution*, by Huberman and Sweezy.

Now imagine as Fidel's troops marched triumphantly into Havana. Suddenly they had to *govern*—a completely new challenge. Even more difficult, they were facing a defunct government that had thrived on fraud and blackmail, and they wanted to start a new government that was fair to the whole population. This was a project that had never before been accomplished in history. The new revolutionaries certainly couldn't look for help in the United States that had been bullying them for fifty years. The current antidote to any "capitalism" was the Communism existing in the Soviet Union. Already, in 1959, the Cuban people were culturally more advanced than the Soviets, and they had many different expectations from their society.

Thus the first thing that the new revolutionary government had to do was to hire knowledgeable, experienced specialists who knew how to govern and who also were in agreement with Fidel's new aims in society. This new government wanted individuals who could direct them "how" to achieve their new goals. Easier said than done. There was a long chain of well-intentioned specialists who fought tooth and nail with each other about the best way to handle every situation. Hindsight is twenty-twenty.

Fidel listened—a lot. But in the end, whoever convinced Fidel and his chosen few at any given moment dictated the next moves. It wasn't unusual for the government to change its mind about how to do something, even in the middle of a project. They claimed they were learning by experience. When I first arrived in Cuba, a heard a lot about the political figures coming and going, ministers being fired, others being promoted and exchanged. I might have understood some of it, like who's who that day, but I didn't really follow the details.

For the real scoop on these political shenanigans, the American economist and author, Maurice Halperin, who was brought to Cuba by Che Guevara to steer the economy, wrote three books about the Cuban economy, step by misstep. Sometimes Maurice upset me with his wise comments, but I guarantee that he got all his facts right. My life just consisted of the daily activities of the ordinary citizen. Throughout my whole stay in Cuba, every person spent his or her whole time complaining about how Fidel "should have" done this, or Fidel "shouldn't have" done that. Good old hindsight. I really don't think there were any simple answers.

When Fidel and his group came into power on January 1, 1959, the old system had been in full function, and the stores were full of all the wonderful things that few people had been able to buy. Then with a stroke of the pen, everyone had jobs, with a corresponding pay schedule. Of course, all workplaces could use extra hands if the government was going to guarantee their salary.

Next, all medical treatment was free, with all salaries to medical-related staff guaranteed.

Then there was the effort to teach every poor person in the country to read and write. Everyone who was renting a home was guaranteed not to be evicted, and empty homes were immediately given to the homeless. Apartments were built for the poor fisherman. All this happened in the first three years of the revolution, just before I arrived. At this point, I called it the "Santa Claus Revolution."

In 1962, when I was first traveling around the city and had time to go downtown, I still saw the big department stores, even with their amazingly noncommercial Christmas decorations, but by then, since everyone had money, people had been able to buy more products than were brought in, so the shelves were empty. The American embargo against Cuba suddenly made the acquisition of all the ordinary items difficult to obtain.

I remember walking into the department stores, with the relatively empty shelves lined with only women's purses and a few luxury items. A couple of years later, these big stores didn't exist. Now there were many, many smaller, local stores carrying dry goods, all with long lines to buy rationed clothing, towels, fabric, and other items. When a product came into the country, it was guaranteed that every single person could buy just one of each item, which was not limited to the few who had the most money. However, many necessities—pens, shampoo, soap, toothpaste, for example—were often scarce, so the economy was not about who had more money, but was the economy of scarcity. How would they measure that?

At the time of the revolution, the middle class was hit the hardest, and the rich were long gone, taking their money with them. These rich huddled in the States, generation after generation waiting for the Cuban politics to "turn around." The poorest people at the beginning of the new regime now had forgotten that they had been poor and had all the aspirations of being middle class. Just the elders really remembered how miserable life had been before 1959.

Cuba had had very little manufacturing previous to the revolution, and the few existing factories often didn't function because they couldn't get American parts for them. The entire previous economy was based on the monoculture of sugar and also depended on the price of sugar each year. Of course, most of the sugar-producing companies were owned by North American corporations, so their lobbyists would keep things sweet with Washington. When the Americans decided not to buy sugar anymore from Cuba, it was definitely a serious drawback.

When the Soviets then offered to buy its sugar, Cuba was not in a position to refuse. Thus Cuba became known as part of the Communist bloc," and although the Cubans didn't really agree to many of the set Communist societies, they had no choice but to play the role. Privately, the Cubans looked at the Russians with disdain, as if they were country hicks with mediocre educations, because the Cubans had, to a great extent, absorbed a lot of the American culture and expectations. The previous Communist Party in Cuba had not received much respect from the population. Most of the previous "Communists" did not play a large part in the new government.

Thus the Cuban economy was an economy of scarcities, and people learned to survive on whatever fate brought them that week. The Cubans recognized that they would have to sacrifice all of these good things for a while until they had more control of their economy, which would be based on hard work. The definition of "a while" was very elastic. How many years of hard sacrifice did we have to endure until there were more items in the stores, and things would "get better"?

Some people who had been originally revolutionary got tired of the scarcities at different times, thinking everything that Fidel did was a big mistake. These people gradually moved to Miami, where there was more selection in the stores. They hoped that life would then be easier. Others were happy to stay in Cuba, to not be evicted from their houses, to not pay income tax. Free day care, guaranteed jobs, and free education were important to those who stayed.

There were many ingenious ways to solve scarcity problems, and I had my own unusual solutions.

My unique survival skills:

Coming home with the weekly rations, Luis had just pulled into the carport in the little red VW.

"Hey boys," I shouted outside, "tonight we are going to have a McDonald's!"

"Yehhh!" they cried as they came running into the opened side wall of the house.

They knew about McDonald's because they had traveled to Canada, and like all kids, it made them excited.

The meat ration had arrived. It was one whole pound a week for four persons. Eight ounces of steak and eight ounces of hamburger. Half of the ground meat would make four patties, and the other four ounces were saved for another meal.

Laughing, the boys helped set the big glass table. No one else in Cuba had McDonald's. This was special.

All right, how did I make hamburgers with the rationed meat in Cuba?

Meat—the four ounces of ground meat was mixed with milk-soaked bread and egg and squashed into four patties.

Mayonnaise didn't exist in Cuba. My dearest book, *Joy of Cooking*, told me how to put juice from lemons, egg, sugar, and salt and dribble cooking oil in the blender to make mayonnaise. Perfect.

Catsup also didn't exist in Cuba. I mixed a couple of tablespoons of the thick tomato paste (occasionally rationed in Cuba), water, vinegar, sugar, salt, and spices, and then boiled and cooled the homemade catsup. Perfect.

Relish—chop fine green pepper and green tomatoes, vinegar, spices, cook.

Once in a while even vinegar was scarce in Cuba. Most of the time I made it with pineapple rinds. However, Murphy's Law was guaranteed. If you wanted to make vinegar, it would turn into wine; if you wanted to make wine, it would turn into vinegar.

Voila, we had McDonald's.

I traded rice for extra flour. Jars of sweetened *fruta bomba* (papaya) made an excellent "apple pie," if I also flavored it with orange and lemon juice. Even visiting Canadians would ask where I got the apples. When squash was available, it made the best pumpkin pies. My friend Rafael, who learned how to make pumpkin pie when they lived with us one year, said he was the only one left in Cuba who could make pumpkin pie.

The counter-economy:

Equality of access to services meant that some reparations and services barely existed in the regular market. Cuba manufactured very little, and food was not as abundant as people had expected. The farmers, of course, tended to eat better than the city folk, and the lucky people who had relatives on farms were helped out in the food situation. A lot of food was exported, particularly to Canada, in order to pay for enough items to keep the infrastructure functioning. The economy as defined internationally, such as GDP, was hardly relevant.

If the economy didn't work, one could always go to the counter economy. That was a polite way of saying the black market. The biggest black market activity was buying food. At an exorbitant price to a farmer, one could get extra chicken, milk, or eggs. Other people "borrowed" items from their workplaces—everything from pencils to car parts, or any other item not too obvious. These were sold on the black market. It was said that if you asked around the right places, you might find anything.

Fortunately we didn't have to "ask around," since we were doctors, these things fell into our laps. Once we met a farmer who could sell us some produce from his little private yard. We asked how much. He pulled out a dresser drawer—full of cash. Then he said, "How about a warm jacket." Of course, Mum was able to bring him one from the Salvation Army in Canada.

During the years that I was in Cuba, the use of US dollars was forbidden. The only currency we ever needed or used were Cuban pesos. On the black market, they said that they would take one US dollar for ten Cuban pesos. Internationally, the peso was worth zero. Trading pesos for dollars didn't help most people, because they couldn't use the dollars anyway.

Personally, besides helping everyone medically, I had my own tradable stock. My mother came to Cuba many times over the years, often twice a year. She loaded her suitcases with everything and anything bought at the Salvation Army and would bring about ten carry-on bags on the airplane. She not only brought me all the little things I wanted (yes, I was privileged) but a lot of secondhand clothing, or fabric, that we could trade for services. Extra things, like instant coffee, shampoo, notebooks, and pens, she would give to her friends free.

I had a wonderful seamstress. She could make anything out of anything; I just had to point to a picture in a magazine. I gave her extra clothing and fabric in trade for her services.

As the years rolled by, household items became worn-out, just as would happen anywhere in the world. Furniture became frayed, mattresses developed holes. In another world, it could be replaced with new furniture, or one could find a repair person in the yellow pages or on the web. There were no yellow pages, nor new furniture for sale. One couldn't go out and buy upholstery fabric to fix a sofa oneself, and if someone else knew how to do it, he couldn't get the material—by normal channels. Thus, keeping a household decent was certainly a challenge, and I couldn't imagine myself living in a hovel falling apart. There was an Empresa Consolidada of furniture in Cuba, but it was all it could do to keep up with reparations in the school, hospitals, offices, and hotels.

There were ways. My beautiful wicker furniture was falling apart. Then a friend had a friend who knew somebody who repaired furniture, and this person was brought to us. Sure enough, he rewove all the chairs to look absolutely new. This man was a true master of the art. He wouldn't charge us. Everyone dedicated themselves to do favors for each other; we would do our share.

The spindly legs on my dark teak dining room chairs were breaking. Modesto, our beloved neighbor, took the chairs home for a week and brought them back like new. He had meticulously whittled down small pieces of scrap wood, glued them in place, and then restained and revarnished the chairs. It was a labor of love.

Once Luis drove our little Volkswagen in front of a bus and really got it squashed up. Fortunately he wasn't harmed, and since the motor was in the back, it was able to limp home. However, it wasn't drivable. For almost a year the poor car sat crumpled up in the driveway. There were no body shops for ordinary people to have their vehicles repaired; cars were not considered a necessity. The state had a number of good body shops for government cars, but even for them, resources were scarce.

One day, we knew somebody who knew somebody else who worked in one of these shops, and our little car was whisked away. One week later it was returned—brand new! I mean really newer than it had ever been. We could not believe how the twisted, torn fenders and bumpers could be straightened out, smoothed out, with absolutely perfect new paint. Undoubtedly, there were some car body artists out there. Free—no one said who did it, no one charged. We were *somebody*, and it was a favor.

My living room sofa and chair were made of yucky light blue vinyl, which got torn and disgusting as the years went by. Once when I was lucky enough to buy a lot of flowered burlap, I made covers that looked good, but slipped if someone sat on them. One day, a friend who was high up in government told us about an upholsterer who fixed furniture for certain people. I was so excited. Rolando, the upholsterer, came to our house, showed us samples of two kinds of vinyl that he had "in stock," so we chose our color. He was not going to be cheap, but, well, okay. Two days later he arrived in the morning and started to work, first peeling off the horrible old blue vinyl. The next day he came and measured everything, then went off to get the material. The third day he didn't come back. The fourth day he didn't return.

The next week we were getting nervous, and we dared to phone his home number. The answer was that they didn't know anything about us and that he wasn't there. Later we discovered that he had been caught pilfering the fabric from his workplace, and he was in jail. For several weeks we thought that we might be caught for engaging in black market activities, but we never heard another word.

Roland, the same as all of the other private entrepreneurs, worked for the Empresa Consolidada of furniture, but helped himself to the materials from the government for his private work. That was the way the system worked, only black market and cheating solved the problems, as the normal system simply did not function. Since almost everyone did this, it was common for everyone to turn a blind eye to this pilfering; it was the way of life. However, if some oddball person wanted to win brownie points with the government, or had some fight with the pilferer, he could report him, and the miscreant was sent to jail. It's amazing how infrequently this happened, and it didn't stop the activity. It was just the risk you took if you needed a part for the car or a plumbing piece. It was "found."

Where the economy didn't work, the counter economy took over. It was extremely widespread and actually worked quite well, but Rolando just wasn't lucky. And

I wasn't lucky. My mother brought me some beautiful, lightweight, patterned orange fabric from Canada, not really upholstery fabric, and I made the covers myself. They looked absolutely fantastic, but just don't try to sit on them. Sit on the wicker.

All of that said, there was another contrasting incident. It was announced that people could get their mattresses repaired by the state for a nominal fee, but you had to sign up on the list. We signed up, along with another forty thousand people in Havana. We didn't have much hope and soon forgot all about it. One year later, a truck came to our house to pick up the mattress, and three days later it was returned—absolutely new! I can't imagine any of the content was original. It just went to show that they had fabulous craftsmen doing some useful things.

Strange restaurant reservations:

The Cuban government kept almost all of the restaurants functioning. It was probably hard enough just keeping them stocked with their necessary supplies. How does one ration restaurant reservations? In the first years in Cuba, when not everyone had lots of pesos, the restaurants were still accessible. For the first time in my life, I was taken to a few high-end restaurants, such as in the penthouses of important buildings and hotels. Quite an experience. My favorite restaurant, bar none, was El Conejito, a brick, British pub-type place, where top chefs could cook rabbit in dozens of tasty menus. Eventually, just about anyone could afford restaurant meals, which greatly enhanced their family's rations. For a number of years people formed long lines for restaurant meals. The lines got longer and longer, so people came in the early morning and waited all day, or they took turns, until the situation was unbearable. Each person could reserve for four people.

Then the government decided to find a new way to make reservations. People could phone the restaurant the previous night to make the reservation. Well, at 10:00 p.m. every night, thousands of people picked up their phones, only to hear endless busy signals. It was like playing a lottery. One could sit there for two hours, redialing over and over (no redial on the telephones), and just maybe, once in a while, one could hear a ring—yes, a reservation! We would make reservations with some other couple; we would invite each other. After a full day's work, who wanted to sit at the phone for two hours, probably for nothing. Sometimes we were rewarded. More than half the people in Havana didn't have phones, so they might do the favor for their phone-owning friends by dialing the telephone for a few hours. Such a silly business.

Sixteen

What's a Tradition?

So it came to pass that my two boys were born in a
country without Christmas.

The Cubans were still used to having their Noche
Buena (Christmas Eve), which was a big family meal, but
the traditions for children had never been regular, and
there were no consistent customs. Some of the children
had Santa Claus come, which could either be on Christmas
Eve, or he would come during the night, and then they
would discover their toys in the morning. It was a mixture
of old family Catholic and new American television.

For many others, the three kings came on January 7,
leaving goodies in their shoes—not a very family affair,
since the adults were back to work. Still other kids had it
both ways!

However, my boys had a mother who was a Christmas
addict, including all of the traditions, and you couldn't

just legislate it out of my soul. Every summer I traded my extra rice for flour and raisins, rationed once a year (since now "Christmas" holidays had been determined to be in July, after the harvest). I saved it all. Whenever visitors were coming from Canada, I begged them to bring just two things: a little bottle of cherry flavoring and little bottles of red and green food coloring. First I would candy citrus fruit rinds. Then I candied green papaya, tasteless on its own, color them with red or green, and they were my cherries. At times I dried pineapple, and then, every year, I made my famous fruitcakes.

Almost every new item bought during the year with the ration book was sneaked away and hidden in a trunk—underwear, clothes, pajamas, some toys—and saved for December. In those days they made sturdy wrapping paper that could be used year after year, with ribbon, no Scotch tape to ruin the paper.

In December, between the fifteenth and twentieth, I put up our four-foot artificial Christmas tree, with those old-fashioned strands of light. If one burned out, the whole chain would burn out. I used the same decorations year after year, from when my parents had arrived. Even the tinsel was carefully reused. So the other thing I begged for from Canada were little tree lightbulbs. Such simple things!

The children would become ecstatic with excitement because they knew that Santa Claus was coming soon. It would be celebrated on the Saturday closest to the twenty-fifth, not on a school day. They played the Bing

"Christmas" day with Mria Teresa (Luis'
mother), Carlos, Luis, Freddie and Satya

Crosby record constantly, admired the tree, and could hardly wait.

Then the night before Christmas, our Cuban family would come and celebrate the traditional Noche Buena dinner with us. Somehow, Papa Louie, their grandfather, would find a ham, and we'd have black bean soup, rice, fried sweet bananas, and any vegetables and salads that were now appearing in the market. We all feasted, finished with fruitcake, and then they went home.

The boys kept wanting to go to bed from six o'clock on: "Isn't it time for bed yet?" The next step was to read

The Night Before Christmas with all the pretty pictures. They didn't understand all of that English, but the paintings were clear, and it was familiar. Finally, the last song on the record player was "Here Comes Santa Claus," and they would scamper to bed as fast as they could.

Midnight, and Satya Claus began her work, wrapping up everything that had accumulated during the year. All the presents under the tree, lights glowing, it was all an impressive sight. The next morning, which seemed to come very early, the boys were up: "Santa Claus came! Yay!"

There was never a question of what they wanted for Christmas. There were no full stores, nothing to entice them. Whatever arrived in the packages (unwrapped very carefully) was wonderful. It was always a glorious morning, laughing and playing. Enough excitement to last for another year.

This continued for several years, until they started school. Eventually, Freddie, now age eight, realized that Santa Claus didn't come to Anita's and Maito's house. I knew that someday I would have to explain to them.

So I started, "You know that Mommy is a Canadian, and Santa Claus is a Canadian tradition."

Pause.

"What is a tradition, Mami?"

"Well, a tradition is like a game that we like to play, that we've been playing for a very long time. Do you want to keep playing it?"

In unison.

"Oh, yes."
"Oh, yes."
So they settled that Christmas was a tradition, and they accepted it the same way the next years.

Not long after, when Freddie was nine years old and Carlos was seven years old, we had a trip to Canada in December.

We stayed at my brother's house with his family. Every house and every window in Canada had lit up Christmas trees, but that was to be expected, after all, this was Canada. My brother gave them money to buy presents for other people, and that was very new. I don't think they had ever had money, or bought anything, let alone for other people, so it was a lot of fun making little lists for little items.

We were living in Abbotsford, near the Seven Oaks Mall, so it was time to take them to see Santa Claus. I asked them, "I'm going to the mall to see Santa Claus. Are you coming with me?"

"Mommy, don't be ridiculous."
"Mommy, you know that Santa Claus isn't true."
"Mommy, don't embarrass us."
"Well," I repeated, "I'm going to see him. Are you coming with me?"

They reluctantly put on their jackets, dragging their feet behind them. We walked down the hill to the Seven Oaks Mall. When I was little, Santa Claus was always in the toy section of the big department stores, but malls were a new invention, so I wasn't sure how things were set up. The main store was Woodward's, so I headed to their toy section; nothing indicated Santa Claus.

"I guess I'll have to ask them where Santa Claus is," I said.

They pulled on my coat, trying to drag me back.

"Mommy, don't embarrass us, there's no Santa Claus."

"You're being stupid."

"That may be, but I'm going to find him."

Since I wasn't familiar with malls, I thought there might be a central area.

"Let's go," I continued.

They trailed along behind, pretending that they didn't know me. We walked out of Woodward's and saw a row of little shops, and sure enough, there was a large space— the first view was of galloping in the air. Reindeer! Then, the sleigh! Then—

The boys stopped. Carlos's eyes got wider and wider, a tear, then more tears started to spill.

"It *is* Santa Claus! He looks just like all the pictures of him!"

Then I knew that I had won—the magic of Christmas!

To this day, Carlos looks back at that old photo: "That was the real Santa Claus." Every year, at the end of November, that forty-year-old still "gets a jolly in his tummy."

The inconvenience in December:

It is not the case that Cuba had ulterior motives in getting rid of Christmas. For a couple of years, they had

Christmas. Economically, however, Christmas time was a Northern Hemisphere rest season, and in Cuba, December was right in the middle of the sugar harvest, which was the most important event of the year. Fidel recognized that everyone deserved this little extended holiday, but December was not convenient, so they decided to put their big celebration after the sugar harvest, for July 26, which was the anniversary of the beginning of the revolutionary activity—the attack on Moncada, Batisita's feared military fort.

The children, of course, had to have a special day to get toys and joys, so it was determined that there would be a special selling of toys in July. There were expensive toys, midpriced toys, and cheapo toys. Each child could buy one of each. But did the kid get the toy he wanted? Whoever went in the door first had first choice, and every child wanted a bicycle. Each store that might cover 120 kids only had two bicycles. For a year or two, there were long lines. That was never fair. Thus, on the previous Friday night, they put the names of all of the families that belonged to that hardware store in a box, shuffled them around, and called out in the names in random order. This was somewhat fair. I know that Raul Castro's children were in the same hat as my children, as we lived in the same area.

Then one year they had another idea. They would do the same as the restaurants—have people phone in to their store, and in the order the calls came in would be the number one had to shop. The calls would be between

10:00 p.m. and midnight. Everyone in Havana managed to be sitting by a telephone at that time. At exactly 10:00 p.m., every phone in Havana was lifted—imagine the chaos. The whole phone system collapsed completely. Occasionally a very few people were able to get through, but I think the telephone system didn't work again for days. I forget how they ended the toy list.

Luckily, it didn't matter to us. We still had Santa Claus.

Seventeen

The Crime Scene

Robbed!

Gone! I blinked, but my eyes were not deceiving me. The clothes were fluttering nicely on the clothesline in back of the house, but there was a hole in the space where my husband's three shirts had been hung. Stolen!

I had been so careful with his shirts. I only hung them out to dry when I was in the house, with doors open so that I could keep watch. Our backyard was surrounded by a chain link fence, which only had a tiny opening at the back of the quarry wall, so the only people who could get there without being obvious were the neighbor's teenage sons. I was certain that they were the ones stealing my husband's shirts. Unfortunately, I couldn't accuse them of anything, as their father was to be my boss in the Ministry of Health.

There was so much robbery that it was an insidious part of the landscape. It was not so much robbery of money, but robbery of simple, useful objects. Clothes could disappear from the clothesline so quickly that a housewife didn't dare leave anything outside without constant vigilance. Even the rotten old buckets used to put out the garbage would disappear if you didn't run out instantly when the garbage truck passed and reclaim your bucket.

In another incident, my mother was alone at the beach, and she needed to go to the restroom. A nice family was parked nearby, parents with two sweet children, and my mother had been chatting with them.

"Could you please keep an eye on my towel for a couple of minutes?" she asked. They happily agreed. When she returned, the family had left, and the towel was gone.

Crime is the bogeyman of every country.

Only the bad guys:
At that time in Cuba, the Western countries viewed Fidel Castro as a bloody tyrant. These Western countries imagined that Cuba had hidden soldiers listening in at every corner, and that if anyone whispered the "wrong" word, he or she was picked up and disappeared forever.

Actually, the opposite was the truth. Before Fidel's time, a president named Batista reigned in Cuba, and he really was a bloodthirsty tyrant. There were hundreds of martyrs—young men who fought against Batista—who were caught and tortured, until they too disappeared. Compared to that regime, Fidel's reign was the most peaceful time possible. It's true, particularly at the beginning of the revolution, that many of the previous soldiers coming down from the mountain continued to proudly wear their green uniforms, but with smiling faces that welcomed everyone they saw. No one was punished for saying something out of place. Of course, if bad guys were actively planning to assassinate Fidel, the perpetrators would be corralled and suffer the consequences. This would be true in any society.

The safest streets in the Western Hemisphere:

Over the past century, particularly in the developed countries, government statistics have kept records of the number of crimes committed each year, so as to be able to claim that the "crime rate" had decreased, or to be forced to organize more crime control. Naturally, murders and significant violent assaults are recorded by the police and the hospitals. Robberies were recorded in areas where there were insurance claims for the losses, but not all countries, or all people, had insurance coverage.

In many countries, rapes were sometimes reported, but unfortunately, this kind of crime was frequently ignored.

In Cuba in the 1950s, there were crime statistics available that indicated that the Cubans suffered from significantly fewer murders and violent assaults than reported in other parts of the world. This lower violent-crime rate in Cuba became the subject for a number of studies by interested psychologists, who concluded that there was less physical crime because little Juanito could take his bottled-up hatred and go home to cry on Mommy's shoulder. Families were very tight knit in Cuba.

This traditional family closeness emphasized respect and important recognition to all children as well as to adults. The disintegration of the family and the abandonment of young people, characteristic of more industrialized countries, had not arrived in Cuba. Each person had a dignified position in the society. Children were the center of the household and were always treated with great respect. If visitors came to our home, they had to say hello to each child, maybe even have a little conversation with them, before continuing with the adult interaction. Children could not be ignored.

In the fifteen years that I worked in a central Havana hospital, either frequently or continually in the emergency ward, I never saw a murder or an attempted murder. Within the entire Cuban emergency system, which had a closed pipeline, I only heard of three cases of useless "family murder suicides"—two were in Havana and one case was in a small town. In all cases the perpetrators were known as schizophrenics. (Schizophrenia is a form of mental illness.) I remember only two cases of senseless stabbing of strangers—one case was at a bus stop in front of another hospital. Again, they were done by mentally ill people.

We did treat a number of gunshot wounds, particularly in the first years, but they were always due to accidents.

After those incidents, Cuba made a point of collecting all the guns that had been used in the revolution, so later we saw very few gunshot incidents.

As for murder, unless the murderer was mentally ill, what motive could there be? There were no more rich people, so someone certainly couldn't kill for money or inheritance. If a guy screwed another's wife, the adulterer would certainly get beaten to a pulp, but there was no reason to kill him. Men did get into fights, and screwing each other's wives was plentiful. I expect a lot of that wasn't reported and didn't get into the hospital system.

Women still have problems:

Rape of strangers in the street was practically unheard of. I used to walk home alone at night, which you could do in any part of the city, without fear of malevolent people. It was customary, not threatening, for strangers to speak to strangers.

However, inappropriate touching of children by family members was probably similar to that in other countries, but possibly less tolerated, as women were less dependent on men as in other places. I never heard of children being kidnapped. What could someone do with them? It was a nosy island, and no one could leave.

Once a Canadian visitor asked me what system we had in Cuba to handle child abuse. At first I didn't know what she was talking about. I finally got the gist of her explanation. Yes, one could spank a child if he were dangerously misbehaving, but I never saw one beaten, tied up, or other strange treatment. Once in a while there might be shaken-baby injuries, but this could not go on very long with a child screaming, because with the noise in open windows, the neighbors didn't hesitate to intervene. These cases were handled individually, by the neighbors, by the CDR, or psychologists treating the offenders. They could be separated from the household if necessary.

Stalking would be next to impossible, with the CDR defense committee keeping an eye on everything. Remember, nobody moved, everyone knew everyone else.

Wife abuse certainly existed, but was treated on an individual basis. Slapping, more rarely punching, happened, and just like in the rest of the world, women often didn't report it. However, it didn't take long for the neighbors to figure it out. If the offender were removed from the household, the wife would often take him back. Unfortunately, this is still typical of wife abuse throughout the world. The guy returns, so sweet and repentant—until the next time. As in many cultures, the Cuban men were paranoid about anything that threatened their "manliness." It was up to us doctors to do our best with reasonable counseling.

Once, while I was working as head of emergency, a woman was brought in for dizziness, and she kept passing out. The tests showed that her blood count was very low with no actual signs of bleeding. She received a transfusion and was sent home. Three days later she was back, with her blood level down again, no black stools, no vomiting blood. What was happening here? With much difficulty, we finally got her to confess that her husband had socked her hard in the stomach. He had broken her spleen, which continued to bleed, resulting in the spleen having to be removed. One nasty doctor commented, "They should teach men to hit their wives in the butt, not the stomach."

There wasn't a special shelter for abused wives. The abused women stayed at home and the husband was removed. As I previously pointed out, everyone knew everyone, so it didn't take long for the neighborhood to intervene if the guy tried to return and "get even." The woman didn't have to be afraid of more violence (unless she took him back), as she didn't have to stay with the man for economic reasons. All women had their jobs, didn't have to worry about rent, and had access to the same cheap food. Their neighbors would not let them suffer.

The women who had worked as prostitutes during the old regime were immediately given jobs or sent to school. They were guaranteed all the rights and privileges available to every Cuban citizen. After 1990, when the almighty dollar was reinstated in Cuba, there were probably women who offered themselves to the tourists, but that was not during my time in Cuba.

Another observation, while I lived in Cuba there was no trace of gang violence. Every single young person either had a job or was studying. The Cubans were adamant that every individual should retain his or her personal dignity. There were no drugs available (except maybe medical drugs) because Cuban money was useless in the outside world. There was no basis on which to profit from gangs and gang warfare.

I do remember that we often passed several fields of hemp on our trips to Varadero, but the hemp was used to make rope. It never occurred to anyone to smoke it.

Still the counter-economy:

There were certain repairmen who could "fix anything," as previously mentioned, men who could actually get parts or materials for repairs. "Taking" something from one's worksite was so common, it was almost considered a job benefit, even though it was usually illegal. Once in a while someone blew the whistle, particularly if the whistle-blower had bad issues with the "borrower," who was then punished. In other words, always keep on the good side of your coworkers, so that this "borrowing" system could continue unhindered.

This "gray" attitude was part of the thriving black market—the only way that the economy could limp along.

Robbery included postal workers taking things from the mail. It was almost impossible to send anything to Cuba from Canada by mail. Even the simplest items, such as calendars, would never arrive. Or the envelopes would arrive empty.

This brings me to the funniest exception. I had never allowed my boys to have guns for toys. One year, when we had Christmas in Canada, Freddie convinced Carlos to buy him a toy cowboy pistol with his gift money. What could I say?

When we arrived at the airport, the security man took out the realistic-looking pistol saying, "You can't take this with you. Even toy guns are not allowed."

Naturally the kids were upset. The nice man took out a big, white paper envelope, inserted the gun and told them, "Give me your address, and I'll mail it to you." Yes, mail it to Cuba. Bye-bye, gun. One year later, with the white paper all ripped apart, when everyone had forgotten all about the incident, the gun arrived!

Eighteen

Year of the Ten Million

Tiring of austerity:

It wasn't long before ten years of the revolution had passed, ten years of "we're working hard, and soon it will be better."

In 1962, we were young, excited, and passionate about a new social experiment to improve our world. I now identified myself as a Cuban when I said "we." We were willing to work hard and to sacrifice immediate luxuries in order to build something grand. We did volunteer work at every moment; we felt that it was worth it. There were scarcities in the food chain, in the household items, and in many daily nuisances such as transportation, but it would be temporary.

Now it was almost the end of 1969, and we were all waiting for the big announcement of the year. The big announcement was the naming of the year, which had been the custom of the Cuban revolution. At the beginning, the Year of Literacy was a great success, where all Cubans pulled themselves up by the bootstraps and learned to read. Then came other years, the Year of Economy, and others that I don't even remember.

Now, ten years later, the young diligent revolutionary youths were having families, and the scarcities were felt harder. Our kids and the future were "now." Weren't we supposed to be "getting there"? When would the hardship end? The positive passion was starting to drag its feet. Ten years ago even the poorest people had expectations of living as the middle class, now those thoughts had faded away. Basic food and shelter were still the issues.

Year of the Ten Million:

It was time for some resounding, big improvement. Then came the announcement: 1970 will be the Year of the Ten Million!

Ten Million what?

Cuba would produce ten million tons of sugar, and the whole economy would turn around. The price of sugar was up, and we had a guaranteed market in the Soviet Union, so every person would get out to the fields and cut every last stem of sugarcane—no matter how many people and how many resources it would take.

Suddenly the returning excitement was palpable. This was something we could really do. We were on a roll!

Throughout history the Cuban economy depended on the production of sugarcane and sugar, which was measured in tons produced per year. During the average, maybe poorer years, Cuba might produce four to five million tons. The government was making a great effort to prepare more land for sugar crop, to plan for more labor, and to cut more cane. Since everyone had permanent jobs now, and there were no unemployed workers waiting for seasonal tasks, sugarcane cutting became the primary volunteer job, decorated with prizes and glory. Cane cutters were our heroes.

The sugar harvest was from the end of November all the way through May. Some groups of people would go out and live in the country for one month; other groups would even go out for three months; and just about everyone took turns working six hours on a Sunday. These volunteers were taken out of their regular jobs for long periods of time, so the remaining workers had to volunteer more than their regular share of work. There was a lot of social pressure to be a volunteer, so you had to have a very good reason not to go out for some hours.

The Soviet Union had signed a contract to buy most of the sugar for five years—and at a price a little higher than the going rate. In order to help improve productivity, the Soviet president, Khrushchev, promised Fidel Castro that his scientists would invent a combine harvester machine that could harvest the cane even more quickly. Khrushchev boasted that if the Soviets were able to go into space, they could certainly invent a machine to cut sugarcane. Cuba and Fidel awaited this marvelous machine, but there were always a few "kinks" in it, and over the years it did not seem to get invented.

The government had set the goal to cut ten million tons, and every Cuban felt that this would be the secret to getting our economy thriving again. Everybody, every individual, took it upon himself and herself to participate in every way possible. There was a positive frenzy, a huge optimism, that we would work hard, we would *do* it, and life would be better. I felt it just like the Cubans. We'd show the world that we could make it.

It just so happened that Luis and I had planned to take a vacation back to Canada that year—an event that took months of organizing. In these infrequent trips, we were able to relax, reconnect with our family and friends, and see how the rest of the world was changing while Cuba stood still.

Among our favorite friends were Maurice and Edith Halperin. They were an elderly couple who had lived in Cuba in the early sixties, when he worked in the Cuban Ministry of the Economy (JUCEPLAN). He was one of the most brilliant people I knew, both highly educated and also worldly wise.

By some coincidence or luck, I was present for their fortieth, fiftieth, and sixtieth wedding anniversaries. He had spent the last thirty years of his life studying the Cuban economy, working with their economists from the Mexican mountains until 1966. He published three books on the topic of the Cuban economy, name by name, blow by blow, every detail of what was "right" and what was "wrong." I spent many years not agreeing with him totally but very aware that all his scholarly facts were undoubtedly correct. He definitely had the facts right, so I highly recommend his books.

"How nice to see you, Edith and Maur," I said because I was ecstatic to greet them on this trip. We were having supper with them in their townhouse cafeteria at the Simon Fraser University, where he was still professor emeritus. Edith poked her pumpkin pie warily. "Do I like this, Maurice?" What a couple!

No, Maurice!

Anyway, when we asked about his work at the university, he grilled us with all his questions about what we were doing in Cuba and medical school at the time.

"They won't make it," declared Maur.

"Won't make what?" I was wary.

"They won't cut ten million tons. They can't do it."

We were aghast.

"How can you say that, Maur? Everyone, but *everyone*, is doing everything to plant and harvest every last stick of cane! Even the doubters are out doing their best to help reach the ten million."

Maur calmly insisted, "They don't have the organization; they don't have enough land; they don't have the policies to cut that much."

I don't need to say how deflated we felt. We agreed to disagree, but secretly we were upset, because we knew that he was still the expert on the Cuban economy.

Right, Maurice:

We returned home to Cuba, cut cane on Sundays, and continued our work. It felt as if the entire population was mobilized.

Cuba didn't make it. No ten million tons. Halperin was right.

Cuba did manage to cut eight and a half million tons, which was more than they had ever cut previously, but it wasn't enough. The world stayed the same.

The grumbling continued. A number of the poorest, who now had their kids in schools, now had medicine, now had shoes, now had electric lights, were better off, and sometimes thankful. In most cases there was still optimism that the economy would improve in the future, but we just had to "get it right." Of course, everyone blamed the Americans with their blockade, or we would have been rich long before this. We had a rich land, agriculture, fish, labor, minerals, and the will to work, and we could compete with the world. We were not happy to be dependent on the Russians.

It is true that the blockade affected the economy. The manufacturing that Cuba had built previously had depended on American parts and repairs, which were not available. It also forced Cuba into the Russian camp.

In those days one had to be either pro-American or Communist. There was no such thing as independence.

On several occasions there were efforts to renew trading with the United States, and we'd get hopeful for a while. Unfortunately the efforts would terminate by the Americans' making a list of demands that, even to apolitical people, were unacceptable. *Asi es la vida.*

Nineteen

Mourning the Little Farm

Papa Louie's perky little farm in the nearby country-side was a fleeting treasure during my Cuban life. I remember the great days. We had nicknamed Luis' father, who was also Luis, Papa Louie.

I boiled one whole gallon of milk in a big aluminum pot on the large electric stove. I had to watch carefully so that it didn't boil over. All milk had to be boiled in Cuba, once when we received it, and if any was left after two days, it had to be reboiled. Such a valuable thing as milk could not be allowed to go sour. When it arrived in bottles from the milkman, the milk was pasteurized, but not homogenized. Now in Canada, I don't know what they do to milk to make it last so long.

Anyway, a gallon of milk was a marvelous gift.

Papa Louie had spent his life being "a manager." He had managed this and that, most recently road construction, but now he was managing a moderate farm close to the city.

It was a beautiful farm—all the crisp green fields were overflowing with an abundance of clean, neat vegetables. The sparkling pigsty had many cubicles with proud sows and their dozens of wiggly, jiggly piglets. The healthy cows gave abundant milk, and the industrious chickens, running everywhere under our feet, laid plenty of eggs. The whole atmosphere was a delight, even for the uninitiated in farming.

That Sunday we had spent the day resting at the farm. We were rocking in the bamboo chairs in the shade of the veranda, drinking beer and eating crackers and enjoying the view, when Papa Louie announced, "We have a new member of our farm, and she's right there."

Right there—she was a goat!

She was a large, peach-colored goat—just like one that I had in my childhood. Standing a few feet from the porch, she appraised us with her wise goat eyes. I had always felt that goats had a great sense of humor.

"The problem is," continued Papa Louie, "that we are having difficulty milking her. Goats definitely are not the same as cows to milk. Their udders are a very different shape."

What do you know! I knew how to milk a goat. In my childhood, we had farmed a homestead in the distant Hudson Bay Mountains in central British Columbia, and the only animals that could withstand the cold with minimal care were sheep and goats. By the age of ten, I had milked lots of goats.

They brought a small, stainless-steel bucket. I found a little bench and perched myself beside the goat. She didn't move as she was probably grateful that someone was going to take the pressure off her udders. *Squirt, squirt, squirt.* I emptied the goat's milk into the container. The goat said thank you and walked off. Amazing! It was the only thing that I knew better than the farmers. I imagine they learned by experience afterward.

The existence of this farm in the family allowed us to receive a little extra milk and vegetables from time to time. Every little bit made a difference in alleviating the struggle to put meals on the table.

Cuba had the perfect climate and soil for fruit and vegetable farming, so it was encouraged in every corner of the country. However, as happens in many developing countries, more of these products were exported than used locally. These vegetables grew best in the cooler season, so most of the harvest was from February through April. We had watercress for salad every month of the year. Citrus fruit grew easily, so the Isle of Pines was cultivated intensively in citrus, becoming one of the best citrus sources in the world. We Cubans rarely, if ever, had the chance to enjoy these fruits. One would have to go to Montreal to eat a Cuban grapefruit. Likewise, our coffee came from Brazil: Cuban coffee was exported for more money.

Two years later, the existing powers decided that Papa Louie should retire and replaced him with some new university agricultural graduates. The university education didn't replace experience, and in no time the little farm literally went to seed. It wasn't kept clean enough; the milk and egg production plummeted; and the plants withered.

Unfortunately this was the case in many of the government farms at the time. The small farms were run down by poor management and lack of experience. The young graduates often did not take well to advice from the older, experienced farmers, who might not be able to read or write, but would shake their heads in dismay. The big sugar-growing coops continued, and the smaller, private farms that had been given to the previous agricultural workers continued to produce satisfactorily. All of the food was harvested, thanks to *trabajo voluntario* (volunteers), but often was not coordinated with the spotty transportation system, and the food would rot. Private farmers would sell "their quota" to the government, but if they produced more, it was not recorded—off to the black market.

Twenty

Our Understated Graduation

The useless party:

You had to like beer. I hated beer.

We had just finished the last step in our long program of drudgery—we were doctors. We had completed one year of premedical courses, five years in medical school, and one year of internship. Each year of Cuban medical school was much more intensive than I've seen in the Canadian programs. Each of the five, not four, years of medicine consisted of eleven months of classes, and that included four years of everyday hands-on contact with real patients, in real hospitals, in real emergency rooms, and in real country clinics. We now felt "ready." We were ready to work.

On the day we had completed our last exam, and we knew that we had passed everything, it was time to celebrate or something.

Such bad luck, I was not to have a flowing black cape. I was not to wear the cute little square black cap. Ever.

When I had graduated from high school, it still wasn't the custom for grade twelve graduates to have a hat and cape. These details were to be saved for those fortunate enough to graduate from a university. For my high school graduation, I was called to the stage often enough—highest marks in mathematics, highest marks in English, and highest marks in graduating class. Enough pomp and ceremony at that time. At least I was able to wear a flashy, gold formal dress.

Graduation from medical school was definitely a time for celebration. However, this was the time, 1970, the Year of the Ten Million, when every resource, every penny, every person was attached to the sugar harvest, so any extra time and energy to put on a party, even a medical graduation, was out of the picture.

So no graduation ceremony. Done, we were doctors. When we finished our last exam, we had to go downtown to notarize our signatures, as happens everywhere, and now we were certified doctors. We didn't need a diploma or any papers to identify us. The government, which would give us our jobs, knew exactly who was available.

Of course, we couldn't be completely ignored. It so happened that at this time in 1970, there was a shortage of beer in Cuba. I had never noticed this shortage, but evidently a large part of the population complained bitterly. Maybe the beer workers were out cutting cane, or maybe the beer was being exported. Anyway, it was severely rationed.

Thus, the highlight of our graduation was to have a free beer party in the beer factory, where we could drink all the beer we wanted.

We weren't very excited when we dressed ourselves for the party that Saturday night, but our friends would be there, so it couldn't be too bad. In our red VW bug, we drove to the outskirts of town where this rambling, wall-less cement structure of a beer factory was located, surrounded by a rusting chain link fence. We were ushered in, parked, and then carefully stepped our way onto the dirty entrance. There were simple uncovered tables and chairs scattered about haphazardly among the large beer vats, and some people were weaving around from place to place. We couldn't even see our friends. The factory felt filthy. There was beer splattered all over the floor, and bits of leftover buffet were strewn around. Ugh. Not a very elegant venue.

"Let's go home," said Luis, and I heartily agreed. So much for university graduation.

Five years later, we were called to the university to pick up our diplomas. There was an old crinkly man who hand wrote each and every university diploma, and evidently he had a three-year backlog. He personally handed each of us our diplomas. To top it off, he always put the date that he was writing it, not the date that we had actually graduated, so even though I graduated in 1970, the diploma said 1973. Since our employer was the Cuban

="3">

government, the officials didn't care about the diploma. They didn't waste any time in allocating our work.

Country medicine:

Now we were packing suitcases in our little car for a two-year stint working in the countryside. This was a voyage only thirty minutes away, but included an absolutely new way of life. Luckily for us, colleagues Rafael Alvarez, and dentist Rosa Maria Delphin, needed a place to stay while they awaited their turn for an apartment. They spent those two years caring for our Havana house while we were away, and got their apartment just when we returned.

Our free medical education had a few strings, or maybe ribbons, attached to it. In return for the free classes, and a minimal money allowance for living expenses, after graduation we were expected to work in the countryside for two years. After those two years were up, we then had the option of studying a specialty. Some doctors were located in their own little hometowns if they came from one.

In our case, since we already had a house in the city, and I suppose out of deference to me, a Canadian, we were placed in a little farming community called Ceiba del Agua, less than an hour's drive from Havana. I was given a job in a four-doctor clinic, which came complete with laboratory and ambulance service. It was a cute little one-story building, with lots of windows looking out on lush trees and natural foliage. Nature at its best, no gardener changing things. The windows were a constant lighthearted respite for the serious problems discussed within. Our patient load consisted of the lovely people working on the nearby private or cooperative farms.

Five minutes from my polyclinic, there was another piece of land, a previous farm, where they housed and trained young men to be fishermen (Columna del Mar). Most young men who didn't want to continue studying, and didn't automatically have a job, were supposed to do a stint in the military. However, instead of teaching them battle tactics, this time was used to train them in specific trades, and in this case, they were to learn about the sea, boats, and fish. This farm had a large central building, which served as offices, kitchen, and dining area where everyone, us included, had all our meals. What great meals, lots of lobster fricassee, and I didn't have to cook or clean!

We were housed in a tiny compartment on the side of a large garage, which probably used to be some servants' quarters. It was separated from the big house with a brick patio and a gracious garden. We had two tiny rooms, enough for a double bed, a shelf, and a makeshift closet. Another room had space enough for two beds for the children, but glowed with lots of windows. I was able to squeeze my apartment-sized clothes washer (terrible thing!) in the bathroom, and that was about it. No fridge, no stove, but I didn't have to cook. We could just plug in a hot water kettle, if we had instant coffee (from Canada).

We stepped out our front door to the tree-enclosed patio, with nature's own plants surrounding. It felt so peaceful and charming. I decorated the little suite with secondhand fabric Mother brought from Canada (good old Sally Ann's), curtains and a closet cover made from an old bedspread, and it felt quite cozy. We lived in this place during the week and returned home to Havana for the weekends.

We had no night schedule; the work was laid back; we worked with good colleagues; and we enjoyed the slower pace. Luis's work was not so demanding either, and the children went to an excellent day care near my clinic. For once, we didn't have to force ourselves to study every spare moment. Nice. We were here for two years.

While we worked in the countryside, we invited some friends to live in the spare bedroom in our Nuevo Vedado house. Rafael was a colleague of mine when we were both specializing in biochemistry. His wife, Rosa Maria, was a dentist, and fifty years later we still keep in contact. It was good for us not to leave the house empty, and it was good for them. They had previously been living in his parents' overcrowded apartment and were on the list for a new apartment, awaiting their turn, so it was a good situation for everyone concerned.

Great patients:

During my stay in the countryside, I saw many interesting patients, particularly the elderly—people sometimes over one hundred years old! Dear Inez, age 104, was a large black lady who walked all over the village, making the lines for food. I would pipe in, "Let her be first, she is over one hundred." And they did. She only complained about her arthritis, but her biggest problem in life was taking care of her little son—he was eighty-nine years old and blind.

Then there was Nicolas, age 105. He came to the doctor for constipation. He was a gentleman, a black man, who would come into the office with his cane and would sit primly and properly, unless he was queried. Then if you asked him, he could recite the whole history of baseball, from the year 1914. He knew every player, every score, and all of their averages. He was an encyclopedia of baseball.

Finally there was Maria, 121 years old, bedridden and brought to the hospital with pneumonia. Her mind was still clear, and she could tell stories. One hundred years before, she had been the mistress of Calixto Garcia, a famous general in the Cuban Spanish war, at the turn of the twentieth century. Unfortunately, she did not survive longer. These people are still little treasures in my memory.

Even though I did not work evenings, there was one Saturday when a nearby clinic asked me to cover a twenty-four-hour call in their tiny hospital. I saw more than fifty people before midnight. Some were simple, but it included stabilizing six cases of severe heart attacks before they could be forwarded to better facilities.

Finally, at 1:00 a.m., just before I could get a few hours of rest in the little doctors' bedroom, a gentleman came in with a terrible rash—chicken pox. His treatment was described for him, and he was prescribed a lotion to put on his body to control the itch. I finally was able to lie down. Two hours later, the nurse had to interrupt me—the chicken pox man was back. He still itched! This time I had him injected with antihistamine. Back to bed, an hour later, another wake-up. The chicken pox man—he *still* itched! I felt like telling him to go home and scratch!

Medicine for the world:

Not all new doctors went to the Cuban countryside. There were other options for some of our colleagues. Then, as it is now, the underdeveloped countries of the world were rife with discontent, internal conflicts, and terrorism. The Western countries liked to blame Fidel and Cuba for exporting revolution. We can't deny that Cuba had been an example to the poverty-stricken peasants and workers in other parts of the world. Cuba may have had some sort of minimal military training for a few Latin Americans, but certainly no more than many other countries send.

However, what Cuba did export were schoolteachers and doctors. The enrollment in the Cuban medical school was very large, limited only by the students' qualifications, so Cuban doctors were sent to any poor country that needed them. From our point of view, if a

Cuban doctor went to Africa for one year, he was put to the top of the list for privileges, such as acquiring a car or a home. The Cuban doctors abroad were basically paid in Cuban money, or even in the country's local money, but all living expenses were covered. A number of our friends participated in these stints and came back with some hair-raising stories.

Pedrito and his friend were sent as surgeons to Ethiopia and Sudan. They related that the injured men came from battles between warring tribes, with no rhyme or reason of someone being right or wrong. Often the fight was over water use. The wounded were brought into the little, open makeshift hospital to be patched up, with neither side of the conflicts taken into account.

Pedrito described the dilemma that, at any given time, they could bring in four critically wounded men, but with only two doctors to operate, two men would be saved and two men might die. How to decide on whom to operate. Which ones were younger? They were all young. Which ones were married? They were all married. Which ones had children? They all had lots of children. The doctors felt that they could only go eeny, meeny, miny, moe to decide who would be saved. After they were saved, these men would go out and fight again. My friends said their work was almost ridiculous.

Another time, one of my cardiology professors, a tall, gentle black man, went to work in Angola. At that time there was a border spat going on between the black Angolans and the white South Africans. Angola had been controlled by Portugal for a while, and when the Portuguese left the country, they left behind a beautiful new hospital with all its equipment. My professor raved about the state-of-the-art electrocardiogram machine.

"And to think," he commented, "it had only been used two or three times!"

"Was it the case that no one ever had heart disease?" we asked. "Or maybe they just didn't live long enough?"

He sighed and thought a bit. "I guess they just didn't live long enough."

Most of my medical colleagues who went abroad went to different parts of Africa.

However, we passed the two years working in the lush countryside. The work itself, in the clinics, was relaxed and in a wonderful atmosphere of camaraderie. There were no "poor people" in that area. All of the children had shoes and decent clothes, and all of them went to school. Everyone had his or her job, and the general feeling was the buzz of excitement. On the weekends we returned to our house in Havana, where we joined Rafael and Rosa Maria who were staying there. It was a very good time in our lives. The children were happy, enjoying their respective schools and day care.

Eventually, the two years were finished, and it was time to return to Havana. Duties accomplished, we were free!

Almost simultaneously Rafael and pregnant Rosa Maria were allocated a classy apartment right in the center of the bustling city. It just had one bedroom, so later on they were able to trade it for a two-bedroom apartment.

In town again:

What did "free" mean? We were free to get any job as a general practitioner. Was that what we wanted? Well, we were also given the option of continuing our studies (more study!) to become specialists. Since we had been studying for so many years, what was three more years? I chose internal medicine, and Luis chose general surgery. I was beginning to feel that I had been in Cuba long enough to "study" the social phenomenon, and maybe it was time to return to Canada. What would I do in Canada? Be a schoolteacher again?

At this point, we still didn't have our diplomas in our hands, because Cuba didn't care if we ever got one. We still made a few trips back to Canada, but the conditions weren't right for us to stay yet. It wouldn't be easy for us to get into a Canadian medical school, or we had to find an alternative way to make a living. It was easiest and most sensible to continue on our hamster wheel of life and continue living in Cuba. The Cubans were still hopeful that their economy would improve soon. Many Cubans had ties to the food in the countryside, and we were lucky because of our ties to Canada.

We were placed in the specialist residencies that we had applied for—Luis was in surgery, and I was in internal medicine. Luckily, but probably due to good central heath planning, Luis and I were both located in the same nearby hospital where we had worked previously—the Clinico Quirurgico. From our home it was a five-minute drive, or a forty-minute walk, with the boys' school half-way in the middle. This was very convenient.

When our night-call schedules coincided, hopefully, our mother-in-law was available to spend the night with the boys. Otherwise, we tried to arrange it so that one or the other of us would be at home. Our call day would begin with normal ward work, then continue on actual emergency room duty all night, followed by the regular ward work the next day. If I was lucky, I could get off work a little earlier, with the extra hour to rush home, wash clothes, clean house, and do the chores before the children came home. The shopping, cooking, planning, and ironing formed a complex survival setup.

The residency consisted of three more years of work and study. The ward work was similar to the routine in my internship: rounds on all the patients in the ward and work in the emergency room on nights. This time I was usually the one in charge of the new students. At this point I also had office hours as a consultant in the nearby clinics. Also endless studying—those books were so big and heavy!

New concepts in primary care:

By this time, Cuba had decided to experiment with a newly structured, community primary care clinic. The area covered by the polyclinic was divided geographically into ten sectors, and each sector would have its own team of three doctors: an internist for treating all adults, a pediatrician for the children, and a gynecologist for women and childbirths. This setup avoided having to have one general practitioner as jack-of-all-trades.

My residency coincided with the first experimental community clinic, which happened to be in my area, so I was able to work there for one year—no night calls! Accompanied by a regular full-time nurse in my office, I catered to all the adults in sector one. Thus patients were supposed to go to the doctor located geographically for their area, but if they complained enough, they could be switched to another doctor in another area.

I loved having a full-time nurse with me. She was a jolly black lady, with a good sense of humor and a terrible allergy to shellfish. In the examining room, while I was examining a patient, she would be filling out the lab requests and the prescriptions for me to sign. Since there were no telephones to make appointments, all the patients more or less arrived at 8:00 a.m. and patiently awaited their turn in order of their arrival.

Of course, while waiting, everyone chatted with anyone, about everything and anything. There was a constant rumble of usually happy voices. My nurse cleaned the patients' ears, cleaned cuts, and performed other nursing chores. Children were seen by the pediatricians. Paps and pregnancies were seen by the gynecologists. The general surgeons and the gynecologists both did gynecological surgery, but the latter were busier with cesareans and childbirth. Patient consultation was always in the morning, and the afternoons were used to visit housebound patients or for the occasional hospital visits to our patients. There were regular hospital doctors, since most general clinic doctors didn't have cars nor were guaranteed transportation from clinic to hospital.

One interesting facet of this experiment was to locate patients who had never been seen by a doctor. We had the names and ages of all the patients in our sector, and we more or less wanted to get in touch with the unseen seniors, in order to introduce ourselves and see if they had problems.

One afternoon we knocked at the door of a tiny walled-in bungalow. A little roly-poly old lady (we knew she was eighty-eight) came to the door. Smiling she said, "Good afternoon, how can I help you?" Cubans were never impolite to strangers.

We answered, "Hello, you know that they've built a new clinic two blocks away, and we are your doctor and your nurse."

"Come right in and have some coffee." These home visits were so much fun.

"Do you have any illnesses or problems that you might worry about?" we asked.

"Ha!" she replied. "I spent the first forty years of my life so sick, I was always at the doctors' offices. Then the last forty years, I've been absolutely healthy, as you see me!"

Sure enough, her blood pressure was perfect. Outside on the high stucco-walled patio, the walls were nailed with tin cans of every shape, painted in every rescued paint color, and each tin was full to the brim with different plants. It just went to show that a garden could be made anywhere.

"It's good to see you so healthy. Keep doing whatever you are doing. A pleasure to meet you." And we left. These were such enjoyable afternoons. Other times we might find bedridden, mentally handicapped patients who required some help when we would organize community resources.

We were also in charge of the employees of the shoe factory in our area, as many of them lived in the nearby apartment buildings.

Working on my thesis;

For my third year of residency, I was back in the hospital, honing my skills in internal medicine. In Cuba, in order to qualify as a specialist, you had to do a complete thesis and defend it as part of the final exams. My thesis was about nutrition and heart disease, in which I read all the published studies that had been done in relation to all nutrients, not just fats and cholesterol. I worked on this thesis steadily for three years, because I found that the work already done and forgotten was astounding.

A central medical library in downtown La Rampa had all the medical magazines collected from 1920 until present, and I spent many hours there. Since I could read in English, Spanish, and French, it was also possible to understand Italian and Portuguese. Also, in spite of all the other scarcities, our hospital libraries still subscribed to a good number of American, British, and Spanish journals, so it was definitely possible to keep up-to-date.

Cuba was not able to have an abundance of all the fancy new equipment, but I think we were better at examining with our hands and ears and just as adept in the art as well as in the science of medicine. Our fingertips and stethoscopes could diagnose many things that I found were difficult for some Canadian doctors.

Another feature in the life of any hospital physician was the weekly visit to the morgue. At that time we were shown all the interesting phenomena discovered in the week's autopsies. Later, in real life, when "melanoma throughout the body" was mentioned, I knew exactly what it looked like. I saw so many livers, I knew exactly what each kind of liver cirrhosis looked like. Later, when we did laparoscopies, I was familiar with what I was seeing.

The three years were intense with my dedication to my thesis. Part of it was doing stress tests on a group of patients with the help of the agreeable and helpful cardiologist Dr. Agramonte. The rest of the time I spent profoundly studying everything that I could find written on my topic.

When the time came for my final exam, my own professor didn't know what to make of the topic on nutrition, as it was not a usual field. Fortunately, another professor had just finished studying nutrition in France, so the thesis was handed to him to evaluate. He thought I had done a great job, so, together with the oral exam, I got very high marks. Now I was an internist. I continued working in the same hospital, but future placement was possible.

Twenty-One

The Peak of My Career

Final professional freedom:

Yay! I'd finished all the obligatory studies (for the moment). I had arrived!

Luckily, I was given a position as internist in the plum hospital—the Clinico Quirurgico, where I had done most of my studies. Luis was also accepted on the surgical team in the same hospital. Now we started getting a higher salary, which, in spite of the scarcities, we were able to easily spend it all. Any luxuries, such as good restaurants, were very expensive, even if it was tricky to get a reservation.

Now that I was at the top of the pyramid in charge of things. I began working as the chief specialist in a separate ward, with residents, interns, and students doing all the grunt work under me. Life was much easier. I still had to do night call every week as one of six specialists, but I was able to sleep more than previously. They would only wake me up after all the interns and residents couldn't solve a problem with an emergency or ward patient, which wasn't that often.

In Cuba, no one worried about medico-legal problems. Once in a while, a patient could truthfully complain of neglect, particularly if someone died, and the complaint was treated seriously by the highest hierarchy group. It could result in reprimand, or even mandatory courses for the physicians or caregivers involved.

I begin my career as nutition speaker:

There was an interesting situation in my first year of being a specialist. The original teaching polyclinic, where I had worked previously, gave morning one-hour courses to all their doctors, residents, and students, and they had heard that I had presented a thesis on nutrition. I was the "final word" on nutrition. They invited me to give their doctors a two-week course on nutrition, one hour every morning, for a total of ten classes. I was delighted. I knew so many amazing, exciting stories of ignorance and detection in the medical field of nutrition. First I had to get permission from the hospital to come in late every day. One nasty little internist, who had been my "specialist teacher" in previous times, wanted to deny me permission. He had no use for nutrition, but the hospital director was happy to let me go for the hour.

Every weekday morning, I arrived at the clinic at 8:00 a.m., to meet with a group of about thirty doctors and nurses. I held them spellbound by describing the perplexing problems that had been presented to nutrition investigators in previous times. I would describe some researcher's frustrations with a problem, his experiments, and then I would finish the class, "And to his amazement, what do you think he saw?"

Silence. Anticipation. "Come to the class tomorrow, and I will tell you what absolutely astounded this researcher." All of the observations and experiments were like mystery stories. That's how I saw them, and that's how I presented them. It felt good that I was able to hold their attention on such a mundane topic.

At the end of the course, one endocrinologist came up to me and said, "All of this information has changed my life!" I didn't ask how, but I was flattered by a lot of positive response.

Now, thirty years after my thesis research, I think that I still know a lot more about some aspects of "cholesterol" than many other lipid specialists, and I would always be willing to challenge them to a debate.

Emergency room stress:
One year later I was offered the post of chief of the emergency ward. This was extremely intense, difficult work, but it had the perk of being from Monday to Friday with no night calls and no weekends. With children, I found that very tempting, so I accepted. Of course, in the emergency room, I had all the levels of students under me,

but I was responsible for keeping my eyes on everything that was happening, and I had to make sure that the students learned something from every patient.

During the duration of my emergency work, there were a few momentous moments when new inventions in medicine proved to be lifesaving, changing the face of medicine forever.

First, one of the most common and serious problems was men coming in with either bleeding or perforated gastrointestinal ulcers. They could have any of a variety of symptoms, but we were quick to make a diagnosis, get all the tests done instantly, and call in the surgeons who could take the patient directly to the operating room. Then they invented Tagamet (cimetidine). Suddenly we could properly treat these ulcers without rushing the bleeder to the operating table. Tagamet put the surgeons out of half their work, but I guess they made it up later by doing hundreds of gastroscopies, which were also invented at that time.

Another thing we saw frequently, usually at three o'clock in the morning, was acute congestive heart failure, when family or ambulance would barrel into the ER carrying patients who were gasping for breath with bubbles in their throat. Heart failure was more difficult to treat in those days—we had digoxin, morphine, and theophylline, and we had a terrible mercurial diuretic that was injected in the muscle. Nevertheless, with difficulty, we saved quite a few.

Then they developed Lasix (furosemide). It was the first really effective diuretic, and even given only orally, it worked extremely rapidly. It is still the gold standard.

The invention of Inderal (propranolol) was another big one. For the first time, we could really control high blood pressure. It was so marvelous, we couldn't imagine anyone not wanting to use it. The drug's use in heart disease was, and still is, somewhat controversial. In the seventies it worked so well that we didn't even want to think about side effects. For a while it was the lone effective drug. All of these inventions definitely made a difference in our medical treatments.

As in all emergency rooms throughout the world, the biggest challenge was lack of beds, both in the emergency room and in the wards. We were always being pushed to move the patients along (to where?). Administration tried everything to make us streamline treatment more quickly to prevent the long lines and backlog.

One very busy day, as I worked in the emergency room, I saw the entrance door open and the hospital director heading toward me. Oh, yes, he wants to speak to me. Oh, yes, he wanted me to get things moving faster.

"Good morning, Dr. Satya. A word with you please."

At that moment, two cardiac arrests took place at the same time. "You take that one, and I'll take this one," I shouted to him. The nurses were hovering quickly. The director didn't have any choice but to participate. I imagine he was fairly nervous, as he wasn't used to cardiac arrests. He was a urologist, not an internist. Eventually the problems were solved and the hectic pace calmed down.

"Yes, you wanted to speak to me?" I queried.

"Forget about it." Exasperated, he walked out.

Then one night, out of the blue, they begged me, "We don't have any specialist on call tonight. Could you please cover the night call just this one time?" Well, I guess so.

However, it happened once again. Then it repeated itself more times. Soon I was not only chief of emergency all day, but again doing night calls as well, which became just too much. I was completely stressed.

One day I arrived at the emergency room and started crying, and crying, and just couldn't stop. The nurses shuffled me into a tiny side room, and they called the director. Somehow I just couldn't face another day in that madhouse, and I guess the director saw it in my face that I was burned out, so I was sent home to sleep. I slept for three days.

Easier cardiology:

In the meantime, Luis was making a big fuss that I was being abused. When I returned to work, I was given a completely different placement. I was to be the resident internist in the cardiology and intensive care unit. I think they invented the position just for me.

This job was the complete opposite of working in emergency. Most of the time in these wards, nothing was happening. Instructions were written up in the morning, the monitors monitored, the nurses nursed, and I could actually sit and read a pocket novel. The students would come by, and everything was explained to them. On the occasions when all hell broke loose, even code blue had its protocol.

In the cardiology unit, there were only four patients at a time. Forget about quiet, the patients and I talked and laughed a lot, often telling little jokes. They even joked about death. Here is one of their favorites:

Juanito died, and flew up to the Pearly Gates, waiting while Saint Peter went through his files (no computers those days).

"Oh, no," said Saint Peter, "look at this list. Look at how many bad things you've done in your life! You can't come to heaven!"

Juanito was crestfallen.

"Ah, wait," continued Saint Peter, "here's one good thing that you did. So I'll make you a deal. You can choose between the capitalist hell or take the Communist hell."

"That's easy. Of course, I'll take the Communist hell."

"Why would you want that?" queried Saint Peter.

"Again easy. When they have the coal, they don't have the matches. When they have the matches, they don't have the shovels. They can never get anything going."

There were seven acute-care hospitals in Havana, and our cardiology unit had the best survival rate. Laughing is living.

My dream job opens:
I was soon to reach the peak of my career. First we spent a couple of years working as specialists in our large hospital.

Then I heard a rumor that they were going to build the first new, permanent primary medicine polyclinic, based on the teaching model where I had worked. The area would be divided into sectors, and the people living in each sector would have three family specialists: internist, pediatrician, and gynecologist. This time, instead of rotating resident doctors, they would now have permanent doctors. This would be the final test of this experimental primary care.

The new building site was to be fifteen minutes walking distance from our house, and the rumors mentioned that I would be chief of medicine. What more could I ask for in this career? There would be opportunities for studies, writing articles, and international travel to primary care conferences. The job was five days a week, no night call. This was the job made in heaven. I'd finally "made it there."

Final considerations:

One spends most of one's youth trying to "get there," whatever that means, as if it were a final goal. Work hard, study hard, finish all the requirements of a career, get a dream job, have a beautiful family, own a great house. I was now "there," but really where was I?

Life in Cuba continued with all its advantages and all its challenges. There was no income tax. There were no mortgages. Health and study were guaranteed, but there still existed a hassle for food and goods. I was luckier than many. I could always holler, "Hey, Mom." It was an inconvenience, but our personal family wasn't suffering much. People still ate, but obtaining food was complicated. Transportation was complicated. What luck that I was to get a job within walking distance.

The passion for sacrifice was losing its luster. One heard a constant, low grumbling among the population: Fidel should have done this; Fidel shouldn't have done that. It's easy to find flaws in the past. All the difficulties were blamed on Fidel. For a number of previous middle-class people, the economy hadn't improved that much. Shortages could be in many forms: toothpaste, soap, toilet paper (thank goodness for the ubiquitous bidets), pens, paper, and even hospital supplies. Swearing at Fidel was common, and Comite de Defensa, who supposedly would "report" negative activities, didn't even pay any attention to the complaints. They were complaining just as much themselves.

The American government still had a stranglehold on all of Cuba's international trade. Thus, most Cubans blamed the Americans, but particularly the aspiring middle class started thinking that Fidel's whole experiment was a mistake.

Did these people remember how life was before the revolution? They remembered the full stores, but did they remember that they were full because most people could not afford to buy the products? Fidel was falling into bad graces, and the economy didn't seem to be moving anywhere.

I had come to Cuba to observe the social experiment; for the time being maybe I'd seen enough. I had to take other factors into consideration. What more could I do?

At this point in life, my biggest concern was about the boys. It was time for them to learn to think independently, to question everything that happened, to be able to disagree with the status quo. This was not happening in Cuba. First of all, there was a dearth of information, all very one-sided, if the powers on top felt like mentioning events at all. The newspapers were scanty—no magazines and hardly any books. This was definitely not my world, nor what I wanted for my children. Every regime tends to show the world only from its perspective, but at least in Canada, a persistent inquirer could find both sides of any story.

I clearly remembered one mind-boggling incident. We were in Canada when the Chinese had their massacre in the Tiananmen Square. This news spread like wildfire in all the headlines and TV in North America. When we got back to Cuba, we found that nobody knew about it. The confrontation was never reported in their news. However, at the same time, there was a huge protest in Venezuela, where people were storming the walls of the American embassy in Caracas. This was never mentioned anywhere in the Canadian news.

Luis and I continually discussed this situation. We now had our diplomas in our hands. It would be another long battle, but we needed to pull up our Cuban roots and return to my home—Canada. We would have to depend on my family, because we would arrive without a Canadian cent but with medical diplomas. Somehow, we would again "get there." As we made plans, we didn't discuss it with the children until the end, although it was not a secret as far as Cuba was concerned. They were always surprised every time that we returned to Cuba from Canada.

The first big hurdle was to get Luis a resident's permit from Canada, which could take more than a year. We didn't want to do anything illegal. We made the decision that the children and I should go first, get ourselves established, and then get Luis's immigrant status papers directly from Canada. The Canadian immigration had all kinds of strange rules about waiting a number of years for this status, which could be hurried by getting a special ministerial permit.

The decision was made.

Already missing my beautiful Cuban front room, I sat down in my comfy rattan chair and prepared myself for the prolonged process of placing a call to my brother, Odell, in Canada. After the preliminary endless discussions with the operator, his phone began to ring—in Canada.

A very curt answer, "Hello, what?" I had never phoned Odell from Cuba before, and we hadn't seen each other for three years, but he sounded like he was in a hurry.

"Hi, Odell. It's Satya. How are you?" We always thought that we had to shout to each other, as the distance was so great.

"I'm fine. What do you want?" Huh, that's all, after all this time?

"We're coming home for good, and I was hoping we could borrow the money from you for the airline tickets. The tickets have to be bought there."

"Yeah, sure, whatever, but give me the details quick." What was wrong with him, no questions, no comments?

"Sorry, the Canadians and the Russians are playing each other right now; they are the finalists in the International Hockey Competition. Ooh, there goes another goal!"

No wonder he didn't have time to talk. World hockey, particularly for Canadians, was more earth-shattering than any phone call from Cuba, no matter what. I understood. Quickly, I gave him the details.

"Thanks," I added, and he returned to his hockey.

On July 6, 1979, I returned to Canada with two children, two suitcases, and one accordion.

Twenty-Two

Ever After

What a shock!

I couldn't believe it. There was no doubt that I was suffering from a severe case of culture shock.

Beneath the clearest blue sky, surrounded by majestic spruce trees and timeless mountains in the distance, I was sitting on a blanket on the cool lawn in Stanley Park.

The boys and I were the guests of honor in a big family picnic with my entire family and many of my previous close friends. It was a happy, laughing group of people, all of them giving me hugs and kisses.

They served lots of food, and they asked questions, but I had even more questions about their last seventeen years. Their children were so big now. However, after the first hour, the men and boys separated to play baseball, and the women started chatting with each other about all of their activities. Suddenly I was out of it. The things they discussed with each other were topics on which I knew absolutely nothing. I couldn't participate anymore. I felt so strange, so lonely. Where was I? I felt as if I didn't know anything about their world—almost like I didn't belong here. I never really was Cuban, now I wasn't even Canadian. Would I have to live in outer space?

I must say, it took three years before I really felt as if I "belonged." I think I even spoke English with a little accent at the beginning

When we arrived, my sister, Heide, whisked us to her house, where we spent two months living on her largesse and adjusting ourselves. Very quickly I decided to investigate the steps to getting a medical license in British Columbia. First, I found out that I would have to work for two years in the British Columbia hospitals, as a trainee, before I could get my license. Second, I found out that I had to apply for the hospital position in September, in order to hopefully get a spot in July. Third, I could not even apply in September until I'd written an international entrance exam, the next to be held in April. Thus if I studied the rest of 1979, I would write the exam in April 1980, allowing me to apply in September 1980 in order to begin working the specified two years in July 1981. Whew! How would I survive all that time with the children?

Without question, I had to pass the April exam first, before thinking of something else, and I had to spend time updating my studies. As a single mother with two children, I qualified for the province's welfare money, which wasn't much, but allowed us to move to a tiny apartment next to the Vancouver hospital. Even though the apartment was very little, I felt as if I were rich. I could go to the stores and buy anything. I supplemented this income with housecleaning and also by giving nutrition courses at night school.

My mother often came over and usually lent me her car. I was able to get a minister's permit so that Luis could join us after the first year. The two boys didn't waste any time. They each got a job delivering newspapers, and very soon the three of us were able to buy our first color television. In order to deliver newspapers they taught themselves to wake up at 5:00 a.m. to work before school. Talk about self-discipline.

Depressing hospital work:

April came, I passed the exam, and thanks to all of my father's connections, I got a position as resident in the Vancouver hospital that July 1980.

My two years' work in the hospital positions were absolutely horrific. I felt as if I was the extraterrestrial ET landed on this planet. My ability to assess a patient was often better than the new young residents, but of course, I couldn't tell them anything. They would never know that I was right until the autopsy results, but probably didn't remember me by then. On the other hand, they had all kinds of scans and tests that I had only vaguely read about. They diagnosed everything with tests.

The first day on the ward, I was desperate to learn how to write a complete physical examination in English, which I hadn't learned in their books. In Spanish, there was a very specific format and words in the proper clinical history, and I had taught my students every word. In English, I knew it existed, but I couldn't find it anywhere.

That first day I studied the other doctors' charts to try to get a hint of how to write a history. Most of their charts were extremely shortcut, and only one fellow seemed to write a complete history, but it was illegible. I think I never did learn, but I learned all the shortcuts.

Not once did any professor, or resident, ask me where I had come from, wonder why my knowledge was slightly different, or even have a friendly chat with me. In fact, I found out that "friendly" wasn't part of their vocabulary. They rarely talked to anyone when they made their rounds. Except for discussing treatments, my colleagues never related to the nurses or any other "lower castes." Two guys might whisper to each other, but there was no chatter. Even passing me in the hallways, their eyes were kept averted, no smiles or nodding acquaintance. Compared to the camaraderie that I'd seen in Cuba, this was like entering an ice palace. No one wanted to help me learn about tests that were second nature for them.

I passed the two years very tired and extremely depressed. The only thing that kept me going was that I owed it to the children, and I didn't know what else to do. Thank goodness, there were one or two good rotations, when they really didn't expect anyone to have prior knowledge.

On top of all these problems, it took over a year to get the Canadian government's permission to bring Luis from Cuba as a resident. Even that took a special Ministerial Permit, even though he was legally a Canadian's husband. He joined our household after the first year, getting little jobs and preparing for his big exam.

At the end of the two years of residency, there was another four-hour exam, which I passed. Then I had my medical license, and I could choose my subsequent path. Even though I had been an internist in Cuba, I was happy to be "just" a family practitioner in Canada. I wouldn't have the students, but part of my job was teaching patients how to live their better lives. This was an indirect teaching assignment.

Within my two-year program, there was a workshop on administration for physicians who wanted to set up their own practice. I participated in a lecture called "How to talk to a banker." I took this to heart.

My own clinic:

My mother was moving to a Vancouver suburb called White Rock where she would live in a cooperative townhouse. I looked at the area and saw a lot of growth in a nearby area called North Delta, which had new houses and the beginning of a new street mall currently in development. Sunshine Hills was a lovely middle-class area, with all the trees preserved, so I immediately thought I would open up a practice in the shopping center. It never even occurred to me to try to join an existing practice.

The first step was to go to a banker for a loan. I had absolutely no equity in anything, but I had my MD. I spoke to the banker the way I had been taught, and voila! I had a loan to construct my own building space. I checked all the lease details with a lawyer. I hired a new young architect (who has since become very famous), hired a contractor with all the details, ordered all the necessary instruments on a lease basis, and put out my shingle. It worked.

I had designed the space as suitable for two doctors, with no space wasted. After the first year, I always had a second person to help share the load. This clinic was my cute little "hole in the wall" for over thirty years. I was absolutely delighted with every type of patient—such a wonderful variety of human beings. They were all, each and every one, a part of my own world.

However, for various reasons, my marriage with Luis did not last long, so I spent a while raising the teenage boys myself. Luis moved to Miami, where much of his other family had arrived, and there he became qualified as a physician, earning his living as a plastic surgeon.

In 1984, in a storybook romance, I met and married John Doerksen, and we are in our thirty-second year of honeymooning. He also had two teenagers, so we were a much bigger family.

I now have four grand boys in Vancouver, two grand girls in Miami, and indirectly two more boys.

In my spare time, in the 1990s, I organized a coalition of environmentalists and participated in talks, forums, and TV programs. After that, I spent three years owning a fashion store for larger sizes, resulting in the issue of improving women's self-esteem, both with a support group and with TV shows and a fashion show for *all* sizes. With this activity I published the book *GET REAL: Every Woman's Guide to Real Size, Real Health, and Real Life.*

Now retired, I amazed myself by becoming a plant lover—dedicating myself to making a show garden, learning photography, and consequently giving garden presentations to garden clubs.

However, my greatest interest is still in the health of society and the health of the planet. I spend many hours studying political science and environmental issues. I was always interested in social well-being, and now I find that saving the planet is part of it. In Canada, our voice is now heard in the Green Party.

Keeping in touch:

Fortunately, I was able to keep some contact with my Cuban friends over the past thirty years, slowly learning about what was happening. During the 1980s, contact with Cuba was somewhat difficult. I continued to correspond with Rafael, who had lived in our house once, and with his new wife, Debora. I would have to find a tourist who was going to Cuba, and then I would send a long letter and a small care package with that individual.

It was up to Debora and Rafael to locate the tourist in Cuba, pick up their package, and also return a long letter. In this manner, we communicated several times a year. From what I understand, the economy was slightly better, although they continued to complain.

"The price of ham is astronomical!" they would say. What! When I was there, we didn't have any option to buy ham.

During the eighties, the American dollar was still not allowed. The Cuban population could only negotiate in their own pesos.

In 1990, my husband, John, and I returned to Cuba. We went on a tour situated in a beach near Havana, and we went with two other couples, so it was mostly a holiday beach vacation, not meant to be too serious. However, we rented an eight-seater van and met up with Debora and Rafael, who took the time off to be with us almost constantly, often doing the driving. Debora was now head of pediatrics in the Pediatric Hospital, and Rafael was now the medical biochemist in charge of laboratories.

We spent time going to parks and beaches, but we were able to visit the homes of a number of my previous colleagues, so that John and our Canadian friends could visit quite a number of Cuban homes. We hardly had time to talk about politics, but everyone made us big meals, and they seemed comfortable.

It wasn't until years later that I realized the Cuban economic situation that existed in Cuba in 1990. I remembered that on that trip my then father-in-law, Papa Louie, kept insisting that I come and see his "garden." I didn't have time, and didn't think much about it. I knew that the back of his house was four feet from the neighboring fence. Anyway, 1990 heralded the year that the Iron Curtain—meaning the Communist countries—fell, converting the previous socialist states into a mishmash of privatization.

At that point, the Soviet economic support ended, and Cuba was left without any economic ties in the world. It was up to the Cubans to support themselves while trying to maintain their advances. Most important food products, such as rice, wheat, and some beans, were all imported and paid for with money from the Soviet Union. For the moment in Cuba, there was definitely a whole caloric food shortage. All food rations were equal, except those increased for pregnant women and children.

The Cuban government couldn't help but notice that Cuba had luscious, fertile land, which was being poorly used but unfortunately dedicated to mono culture. To immediately increase food production, everyone was encouraged to plant every little spare space of ground with food, and everyone received seeds, plants, and rotted manure for fertilizer, and for larger plots of land, tractors and oxen were lent to the growers.

Now I know why my father-in-law wanted me to see his garden. He was growing food crops in a vacant lot behind his house. During that trip, I was not aware of that significance. Electricity depended on the oil shipments, which decreased, but it wasn't long before Cuba was getting oil from Venezuela, very cheaply, but basically as an exchange for doctors, teachers, and other technologists.

Shortly after our trip, in the early 1990s, Cuba changed its rules about the use of American dollars in Cuba. In order to get more dollars flowing into Cuba, they allowed ordinary citizens to receive, own, and use American dollars. These dollars could be used in special stores with items not ordinarily available, but for the regular Cuban, prices were *exceedingly* expensive. The Cubans were used to prices set in the 1960s and had seen no inflation, so the 1990 prices were unbelievable to them.

Before 1990, the richest people in Cuba, the ones who drove all those old cars, were the farmers. Now the "richest" people were the ones who had "dollars," who turned out to be those working with tourists.

Other sources of dollars for Cubans were the remissions from families out of the country. It was easy to send money to them from one bank to another. At that time, my friend Debora, one of the top pediatricians and geneticists in the world, would come home from work, fire up her old-fashioned oven, and make cupcakes, which she would sell for fifteen cents each in order to get American money. It got so that, from time to time, I would send them a check of a couple of hundred dollars to tide them over. By this time, email was becoming useful. Most Cubans did not have access to computers or Internet, but she was important in the medical world, so she had access.

It became easier for Cubans to travel, from Cuba's point of view. However, it was not always easy to get a temporary visa in the countries they wished to visit. Canada was just as bad. I had to turn cartwheels at the Canadian embassies in order to bring Rafael and Debora just for a visit to my house. This has not changed in Canada. My sister has a step-granddaughter in Cuba, whom she wanted to bring here for vacations, but twice Canada has refused her visiting visas.

Two-way travel between Miami and Cuba has been abundant and rampant for many years, but as I write this, the economic blockade has fallen, and there is now regular travel between Cuba and the United States. This will see a big change in both countries.

It has been sixty years now since Fidel Castro and I sat on Bertha's cool deck late at night, discussing our respective ideas. Fidel and I, once starry-eyed youths, are now old. He and I were dreamers, passionate about the possibility of making a better world. We imagined a thriving, equal society, where fear and greed were not the guiding factors. I am sure that the Cubans knew that Fidel did not intend to enrich himself, nor to simply enjoy a power trip. I definitely knew where he lived, what houses he had, and where Raul and others lived in our local neighborhoods. He did not live in the palace, where previous leaders had lived, nor invest in personal extravagance as other foreign leaders have.

I reminisce about Fidel:

Fidel was immensely charismatic, a spellbinding orator, with idealistic visions for sovereignty and independence for the Cuban people. In North America, Fidel was often depicted as a tyrant ruling with fear. Nothing is further from the truth. There are so many incidents—many were recorded—that confirm what I saw: a man with great compassion but also great determination. Was he a dictator? He always had a "cabinet" of smart people to help him guide the government, and we know that he listened a lot, but in a group of leaders, it is difficult for any three people to agree on almost anything. Someone had to finally say "that's that."

Did he put people in jail who disagreed with him? If he did that, at some time or another, everyone in Cuba would have been in jail. However, his security services certainly were able to nip in the bud the hundreds of planned assassinations. He was not going to let Cuba fall backward, as in the case of Allende in Chile, or the CIA takeovers that took place in a number of other Latin countries. Amazingly, I calculate that he is now ninety years old.

In those sixty years, it was easy to have marvelous ideas, but not so easy to know how to carry them out. Many individuals called us naive. In the outer world, there was a general consensus that someone couldn't just go out and "change the world."

The world had only been transformed to capitalism and corporatism in the last couple of hundred years. These were considered an integral, permanent condition of increased technology. The only alternatives that society offered were capitalism, socialism, or its extreme, Communism. Fidel wanted to go his own way, but he had to choose between these two extremes. Economically at that time, there was no third alternative. Also, there was no map for his desired economy. Every action had an unexpected reaction, but one had to forge ahead, always making changes with every conflict, trying to improve "mistakes."

I watched all the changes that were made in Cuba, either being there or keeping in touch with my friends. What about Fidel's and my dreams?

Without doubt, many good things happened and some not-so-good things happened. In the long run, comparing it to the progress in the rest of the developing world, I am still very pleased. I can safely assert that compassion was a key factor. Since I had gone with an open mind, even though I had a dream, I was not disappointed because I did not have specific expectations. I feel good that the Cubans have managed to survive with their marvelous education, their health care system, their efforts to eradicate severe poverty, and, most of all, their ability to maintain every individual's dignity.

Today, as I finish my Cuban memories, our mother earth is in a precarious situation. If we don't make a drastic change, we will be no more. Too many people think that it is impossible to make drastic changes. They say, "We can't rock the boat." Do we think that there are only two options: corporate-capitalism or socialism? Cuba taught me that the world can change very quickly if we all become aware of our dangers.

So let there be dreamers. I hear them. I read their books. They are out there. Don't be afraid to dream of a better world, and then *demand* it of your leaders. There are now feasible options: a new economy. (Google it.) The same issue that started the Cuban Revolution, that every person should have equality in life (and *equality* doesn't mean *same*), is still one of the world's biggest issues. In order to not destroy our earth, the top 10 percent of the wealthy will resist vehemently, but the dreamers will show us the road.

Cuba has shown us that, in spite of so many trials and tribulations, one can move forward, attempt to save our earth, and to give all people the dignity with which they are born. Let there be dreamers.

Fidel Castro's famously said in his self-defense in a trial in 1953,

"History will absolve me."

89293388R00152

Made in the USA
Columbia, SC
12 February 2018